HIG...
THE W...ᴌS

HIGH ON THE WALLS

AN ANTHOLOGY CELEBRATING
TWENTY-FIVE YEARS OF
POETRY READINGS AT
MORDEN TOWER

*

**edited by
Gordon Brown**

MORDEN TOWER
in association with
BLOODAXE BOOKS

First published in 1990
by Morden Tower/Bloodaxe Books Ltd.
P.O. Box 1SN
Newcastle upon Tyne NE99 1SN

Morden Tower and Bloodaxe Books Ltd.
acknowledge the financial assistance
of Northern Arts.

ISBN 1 85224 148 9

Cover by East Orange
Cover photograph of Morden Tower angel by Hailey Redgrave
Typography by John Wardle

Typesetting by Bryan Williamson, Darwen, Lancashire
Printed in Great Britain by
Billing & Sons Limited, Worcester.

CONTENTS

Acknowledgements

Tom Pickard's 'Serving My Time to a Trade' first appeared (in a longer version) in the magazine 'Paideuma' published by the University of Maine, Orono, in 1980.

'What the Chairman Told Tom' © Basil Bunting 1978, is reprinted from Basil Bunting's 'Collected Poems' (1978) by permission of Oxford University Press.

'Cattle Show' by Hugh MacDiarmid is reprinted by arrangement with Martin Brian & O'Keeffe Ltd, Publishers, and by kind permission of Dr Michael Grieve.

'What the Sea Throws Up At Vlissengen' by Allen Ginsberg first appeared in the 'American Poetry Review'.

'The Levels' by Jon Silkin first appeared in 'Staple' magazine.

It has not always been possible after such a lapse of time to establish correct credit for some photographs reproduced here, although every effort has been made to do so. We apologise for any errors or omissions in this respect.

PREFACE

Gordon Brown

MORDEN TOWER was built in about 1280 and stands on the longest remaining stretch of the city walls of Newcastle upon Tyne. In 1620 the Company of Plumbers, Plasterers and Glaziers, who had occupied the tower since 1536, added another storey to the building, and this forms the poetry reading room of today. It was here in 1964 that Connie and Tom Pickard organised the first reading. Basil Bunting, who gave the first public reading of 'Briggflatts' at the Tower, thought the readings might last about two years. He was wrong. Amazingly, the readings have gone on year after year and the Morden Tower has become internationally famous. This anthology celebrates those twenty-five years by bringing together work (unpublished, with only one or two exceptions) by some of the three hundred or so poets who have read at the Tower.

In the early days the Tower was flanked on one side by a bus station, and on the other by the backs of a row of nineteenth-century buildings occupied by small factories and night clubs. Now, the area occupied by the bus station has been opened up and grassed over. The factories are long gone, but the same buildings have become the centre of Newcastle's burgeoning 'Chinatown'. Internally there has been little change, except that there is now electric light and the audience sit on chairs instead of the floor. The very simple architecture of the room and its intimate scale – it is roughly circular, and holds eighty people at most – have through the years ensured for poets a space and an atmosphere in which they have been able to achieve a direct communication with their audience. Anyone who has had the good fortune to hear Basil Bunting, Anne Waldman, Allen Ginsberg, Fleur Adcock, Ted Hughes, Robert Bly, Hugh MacDiarmid, Adrian Mitchell and many others read at Morden Tower will have a lasting impression of what is meant by the 'authentic voice' of poetry. Poets and audiences alike have always been aware of involvement in something greater than just a 'performance' in a superficial sense.

Those who came after Tom and Connie as organisers have managed to retain the original anarchic spirit, almost completely free from the dead hand of authority. They include David Westerley, Ric Caddel, George Charlton, Nick Baumfield, John Byrne, Bob Lawson, Neil Astley, Michael Blackburn, Sandy Anderson, Peter Bennet, and lately, for three and a half years, Brendan Cleary.

Many people, as well as the poets, have helped me bring this anthology together. I wish to thank especially Connie Pickard and Tom Pickard, Brendan Cleary, Peter Hodgkiss, Ric Caddel, David James, Derek Smith and Alan Brown; the staffs of Bloodaxe Books, Newcastle Public Library and the Literary and Philosophical Society; and Jenny Attala of Northern Arts. I also wish to thank John Wardle, Matthew Caley and Neil Astley for their unfailing co-operation at all stages. However, responsibility for the final result is mine alone.

Since very early on, Morden Tower readings have been supported by Northern Arts, as is the publication of this book.

BEGINNINGS

Connie Pickard

ON THE 30th March 1964 I took out a lease on the Morden Tower. It was to be used as a book room for poetry readings and discussions. Tom Pickard and I had been looking for an interesting space for books and readings. What we dreamed of was an inviting cellar in an old Georgian house, a little cove of our own where we could deposit the hoard of little press publications, slim volumes and magazines we had collected, where people like ourselves could browse and be in touch with writing from Edinburgh, Paris, San Francisco, Greenwich Village, Liverpool and Ladbroke Grove. But what did I do? I hired a medieval tower.

We spoke to publishers' representatives. Traditional ones would not really entertain us as a viable entity at all, but John Calder's man (who at first tried to persuade us to keep pigeons instead) let us have loads of marvellous books on sale or return. We then set about organising readings.

In those days poetry readings were a matter of Arts Council sponsored tours by BBC Third Programme personages, attended by ladies in flowery hats, and usually took place in Morpeth or Hexham. There was no way you could imagine flowery hats in Back Stowell Street where the Morden Tower stood. This was no medieval lane, but a memorial to 19th century speculation and economy. You could almost lean out of the Tower window and touch the factory wall opposite. I don't know what kind of emissions came out of that place, but they were certainly breathtaking. They died down towards the evening, to be followed by emissions of another kind which were tied in neat semi-transparent packages and festooned the garlands of rusty barbed wire.

So where did we get our audience? In those days there was a floating underground of teachers, civil servants, doctors and juvenile delinquents. They wrote poetry and plays, played jazz, exhibited their paintings in the basements of pubs, sang folk songs, acted in old converted churches and went on Ban-the-Bomb marches. Newcastle was a very hard-hearted city and most of them finally had to go south to spread their wings.

Going to the Tower was not an activity for the genteel or faint-hearted. One poet was deterred at the very last minute. He was part of a duo from Scotland. When he arrived at the entrance to Back Stowell Street he muttered something about a 'hole in the wall' through his beard, turned around and got the next bus back to Scotland in high dudgeon.

He was right about the 'hole in the wall', but for some poets this was part of its charm, this narrow curving lane which you could disappear into like Jesse James and his gang vanishing into a cleft in the rock. And if you didn't keep your eyes peeled you could easily miss the narrow postern door in the wall which leads you to the stone steps up to the Tower.

Once inside you did not sink into a cosy armchair but took your place on the floor, or you could sit on the stone ledge which runs round the walls. If you were lucky, you might get a cushion.

*   *   *

When Tom first went out to see Basil Bunting at his home in Wylam, up the Tyne valley, bearing greetings from Jonathan Williams, we had already booked Pete Brown to open the Tower by reading on the 16th June (Bloomsday, although we didn't know it then). We asked Basil to give the second reading, but he was reluctant. We finally managed to persuade him. At that time he was not writing, having fallen silent after 'The Spoils' (1951). I really believe the warm reception the youngsters at the Tower gave to 'Chomei', 'Villon', 'Let them Remember Samangan' stimulated him into re-starting.

Basil introduced us to the work of his contemporaries Louis Zukofsky, Hugh MacDiarmid and William Carlos Williams. Tom became intoxicated with Zukofsky's 'A' and could hardly wash his face without breaking into 'Ode to my washstand'. At that time I remember the road was up outside our flat and the workmen had placed around the workings those little red and white trestles with red and white poles to mark off the area. So we used to run down the street shouting

> Horses: who will do it? out of manes? Words
> Will do it, out of manes, out of airs, but
> They have no manes, so there are no airs, birds
> Of words, from me to them no singing gut.
> For they have no eyes, for their legs are wood,
> For their stomachs are logs with print on them;
> Blood red, red lamps hang from necks or where could
> Be necks, two legs stand A, four together M.

The excitement being in the fact that such ordinary everyday things were occasions for poetry.

When the readings started to go very well over the first few weeks, Basil drew us up sharply and said…you must not get carried away and put too much of your hopes on this…these things usually have a short duration. He gave the Tower one or at most two years.

Tom and I were living in an old flat in Jesmond. We had a small room which contained a bed, a cot for our son Matthew, a small table and a small cast iron fireplace in which we kept a small coal fire. The walls were of that now most coveted 'distressed plaster' or even plasterless appearance. Tom wrote out Blake's lines above the fireplace: 'Arise and drink your bliss/For everything that lives is holy.' This had quite a tonic effect and I would recommend it to anyone in similar circumstances.

When Robert Creeley came to the Tower in the autumn of 1964 half the School of Fine Art at the University came along with Richard Hamilton to hear him. They were interested in Black Mountain poets and painters.

The early months were probably the most exciting. There were young poets from Edinburgh, Liverpool, Notting Hill or wherever hitching to Newcastle, giving a reading, and dossing down wherever they could afterwards. Poets like Pete Brown, Brian Patten, Spike Hawkins, Alan Jackson, Tony Jackson, were not in the least academic, none of them had been to university, and there was a strong feeling of this being an underground movement. Pete Brown was the real resistance worker and kept people in touch with one another. There were fellow-travellers like Michael Shayer, Gael Turnbull, Malcolm Rutherford, Claud Rawson, helping it all along.

* * *

We had to move as Matthew was getting bigger and needed his own space. I found a very cheap ground floor flat (I was still doing supply teaching so could take on leases and things.) Once we had a place of our own Tom wanted to do something for Baz. At that time Basil was having a lot of trouble with his eyes. He had a job sub-editing the financial page of a local newspaper which required him to read yards and yards of small print. On top of that he was being threatened with a foreclosure on the mortgage on his house. Tom prepared a leaflet about Basil and we circulated it to as many poets as we knew, to let them know he was alive and well. But Tom was really longing to publish 'The Spoils' – and I was keen to start a magazine. After Basil went back to work we really leaned on Richard Hamilton to help us with publishing. Even though he was very busy – going back and forwards to the States as well as doing his own work – he took on both the book and the magazine (which we decided to call 'King Ida's Watch Chain') – a big work-load. Only one issue of the magazine ever appeared. It was devoted to Basil.

* * *

One of the hazards of reading at the Tower in those first few years was that the poet had to sleep in the spare bed of whatever flat, shack, palace, joint or hovel that we had managed to rent or squat in. We roamed like gypsies all over Northumberland and Durham during those first ten to twelve years.

When we finally persuaded Elaine Feinstein to come and read at the Tower we were living in one of the old Scotch Halls on the moors above Allendale. These were originally old sheals or sheilings, used by shepherds during the winter. They had later been made into smallholdings by the lead-miners, who needed both outlets to earn a living. There was a track part of the way, then you covered the rest of the distance by walking over two fields. We couldn't have survived there at all if a friend hadn't given us an old landrover – blue, with a canvas hood. We got used to the rigours of this life. The water was pumped from the bottom of the hill, but we did have electricity (when we could pay for it). And, miraculously, there was a phone. I rarely got into Newcastle for the readings at that time – Matthew did not like poetry in the least. So I usually stayed at home and brewed up the sorrel soup or nettle broth or whatever was in season. It was on the proverbially dark and stormy night when I heard the landrover draw up and Tom tap on the pane for me to answer the door while he parked the old jalopy. I shall never forget the look on Elaine Feinstein's face when she came in. She barely spoke to us. She had come up from Cambridge that day in her city clothes, read in a medieval tower, and been driven over thirty miles in a gale to Wuthering Heights. She sat by the fire, those enormous eyes giving us great baleful glances while I tiptoed about and hovered over the cauldron of woeful stew. I don't think she said much the following morning either. In fact when we met again in more comfortable surroundings and she offered us splendid hospitality in Cambridge, we never really talked about it.

*　　　*　　　*

Early in 1965 I bought that spare bed, a single divan bed from an auctioneer's in Newcastle called Anderson & Garland. At first it stood in the front room at Eslington Terrace bedecked with cushions so that it could be used as a seat during the day. As we travelled hither and thither throughout the sixties and early seventies we lost most of our possessions, but this bed somehow accompanied us. There was a time when it stood in the fields above Allendale for several weeks after the bailiffs had been, rather like the monolith in '2001'. Tom and I reckoned that by 1973 about two hundred poets had slept on it, and that is not counting Walt Whitman, who by some unusual variation of the apostolic succession had indeed by proxy slept there. And what happened to it? This is a mystery. I only know it vanished round about 1973. Maybe Scotty beamed it back to the Moon. Don't ask me.

SERVING MY TIME TO A TRADE

Tom Pickard

IN 1963, along with thousands of other Tyneside teenagers, I was signing on the dole. We had finished secondary education at the age of fourteen or fifteen, and were headed for the army or the cheap labour market. Most of us were unprepared for the sudden and enforced 'leisure' of unemployment. We were sullen and resentful, angry and confused and justifiably so, just as the new young unemployed have even more reason to be.

We turned up each week to join the tail-end of a queue which went out of the Youth Employment Bureau building and round the corner of Ellison Place. We grumbled amongst ourselves and at times discussed setting up a kind of union to deal with employers who took advantage of our vulnerability: 'the bank of human capital,' as one local politician with an Orwellian turn of phrase called us.

At that time Basil Bunting was working as a sub-editor on the 'Evening Chronicle'. His job was to produce the city page for the paper: a dreary and painful task for a man with Mr B's vision. His physical sight was deteriorating and he wore glasses as thick as a safe door. Some years previously he had worked for the publishing firm of Thomas Reed and Son, proofreading bus and train time-tables. He lived in a large sparsely furnished house overlooking the River Tyne at Wylam, ten miles west of Newcastle.

We were a small group of young socialists, anarchists, and Trotskyists and our concerns went towards vegetarianism and yoga, but focused on the CND and its more militant off-shoot, the Committee of One Hundred. We started a magazine 'Eruption' (my preference had been 'Erection', but it was voted down) with Roy Robertson and Tony Jackson. Tony was eighteen but looked thirty-five, South Shields Jewish, bushy black beard and balding. He looked the spitting image of Allen Ginsberg and wrote long marvellous angry poems and listened to Charlie Mingus: Black Saint and the Sinner Lady.

Through a newspaper I discovered a small press publisher, John Rolph of Scorpion Press, situated in Lowestoft. I hitch-hiked to see him. He showed me the large stock of City Lights books which they distributed and gave me a few of the early numbers of 'Kulture'.

Returning home and reading through an issue of 'Kulture' I discovered an advertisement for Jargon Press and wrote off immediately to North Carolina and got back a helpful letter from Jonathan Williams saying he'd recently been to Newcastle and had met a number of persons whom we might want to get in touch with. Their addresses were enclosed and Basil Bunting's was amongst them.

We meanwhile were in the process of hiring a medieval tower on the old city walls from Newcastle Corporation. The tower had previously been occupied by the Northumbrian Pipers Association and later by a group of jazz musicians, both of whom had found it too draughty. It was situated in a long, dirty, dark lane overhung on one side by medieval parapets and on the other by factories which emitted foul and noxious fumes all day. A decaying city has many potentials.

One Sunday night shortly after receiving Jonathan's letter, I decided to look up Mr Bunting in the telephone directory, and I gave him a ring from a public box. His Persian wife Sima answered the call, then sent Basil to the phone. Nervously I explained that I was putting together a magazine and wanted some contributions from him. He invited me over, and I caught the next train out.

He approved our plans to open the Morden Tower and offered what help he could give. We did not realise then just what a struggle it would prove to be. I sat happily listening to 'The Spoils', understanding only a little of its meaning but enjoying the sounds the words made and the undoubted skill with which they were knitted together. It is difficult to explain the emotion felt at hearing for the first time a great and accomplished work read by its author. I was a virgin and stunned by it. The experience was moving and revealing. His tongue was an instrument and rolled each word around as though it were a piece of sculpture. He talked of Persia, America, and Italy, and of course their poets. When he asked if I wrote poetry myself, I confessed I did but had not taken any to show him, out of shyness. 'Well, you must come again, and bring your poems along.'

It was getting late and time to leave. We shook hands and parted on the doorstep. The dark, dewy night smelt river-rich. I could hear the Tyne taking breath beneath the bridge. While standing on the platform awaiting the train, half drunk, I began to go over the poem:

Man's life so little worth,
do we fear to take or lose it?
No ill companion on a journey, Death
lays his purse on the table and opens the wine.

In the distance I could see the small lights of the approaching train and the air smelt sweet. I read it at home many times, hearing Basil's resonant voice.

By a strange coincidence which occurred while I was hitch-hiking to Lowestoft, I was given a lift by a young film maker, who was directing documentaries for the National Coal Board. When I told him of our plans to open the Morden Tower, he suggested we invite his friend the poet Pete Brown. He gave me Brown's address and I sent an invitation. Someone in the Arts School (where Richard Hamilton was teaching) designed and silk screened a poster, which I placed in pubs and shop windows throughout the town. Pete Brown arrived half an hour before the advertised reading, looking like a small bearded bear with its head in a beehive of stinging bees. In fact, he had just fallen sleepily out of a lorry which had given him a lift from London. After two bottles of Newcastle Brown Ale and a couple of strange looking pills, he became very lively and gave a decent performance. The reading attracted a number of young poets and artists. Afterwards we went to the Downbeat to hear the Alan Price Combo (which later became the Animals) and danced all night.

Basil, a few weeks later, gave the next reading and we had a packed house, maybe seventy people. The audience was mainly young. There were students, grammar school kids, apprentices and the unemployed. We charged less money, or nothing, to those like myself on the dole. The young people loved him and were attentive. We listened carefully, not always understanding, but hearing. We recognised and respected this sailor come home. He sat by gas-light (we had no electricity then), his safe-door glasses gleaming, and he read (for the first time in how many years?) to a young audience, who literally sat at his feet (we couldn't afford chairs and besides they took up precious space).

Our ears and hearts were open to the fine mellow instrument of his voice and the authenticity of the experience it sang of. The sailor had found his fireplace and sang fine tunes to freshly awakened ears. Once more his old songs danced like well-made boats on the ocean. After the reading, in the Northumberland Arms, Basil introduced me to the 'dog's nose', a pint of beer with a gin in it. A few of my friends from the dole crowded around and asked questions. They seemed to be spending more and more time in police-cells for increasingly obscure reasons and recognised in 'Villon' (which Basil had read) the voice of experience.

I think because of Basil's presence we were able to attract many good American poets to give readings in the tower, and he was generally pleased to see them. But the poet whom he enjoyed meeting most was Hugh MacDiarmid.

On the way to the tower in a taxi, Basil told MacDiarmid that he was the finest Scottish poet since Burns, and MacDiarmid, chuckling, agreed. Both men had known and respected each other's work, but had never met. MacDiarmid read, amongst other things, the beautiful 'Island Funeral', and after the reading we went back to our flat. The old men were bubbling with the Glenfiddick Fire Water and the youngsters blissful on beer and marijuana.

Mischief sparkled in their eyes all night long, and Bunting sang from his seemingly endless repertoire of bawdy songs.

[1979]

BASIL BUNTING

I feel that a Northumbrian who is a poet has very much a job to do in Northumbria. I'm very glad in my old age to be back where I was born and in much closer touch with the underlying spirit of the place.

BASIL BUNTING/What the Chairman Told Tom

Poetry? It's a hobby.
I run model trains.
Mr Shaw there breeds pigeons.

It's not work. You dont sweat.
Nobody pays for it.
You could advertise soap.

Art, that's opera; or repertory –
The Desert Song.
Nancy was in the chorus.

But to ask for twelve pounds a week –
married, aren't you? –
you've got a nerve.

How could I look a bus conductor
in the face
if I paid you twelve pounds?

Who says it's poetry, anyhow?
My ten year old
can do it and rhyme.

I get three thousand and expenses,
a car, vouchers,
but I'm an accountant.

They do what I tell them,
my company.
What do you do?

Nasty little words, nasty long words,
it's unhealthy.
I want to wash when I meet a poet.

They're Reds, addicts,
all delinquents.
What you write is rot.

Mr Hines says so, and he's a schoolteacher,
he ought to know.
Go and find work.

1965

HUGH MacDIARMID

I have given poetry readings and talks about poetry all over Europe and in Canada, America and China, but never in a place was I happier to be in than the Morden Tower.

HUGH MACDIARMID/Cattle Show

I shall go among red faces and virile voices,
See stylish sheep, with fine heads and well-wooled,
And great bulls mellow to the touch,
Brood mares of marvellous approach, and geldings
With sharp and flinty bones and silken hair.

And through th' enclosure draped in red and gold
I shall pass on to spheres more vivid yet
Where countesses' coque feathers gleam and glow
And, swathed in silks, the painted ladies are
Whose laughter plays like summer lightning there.

Stony Limits and Other Poems (1934)

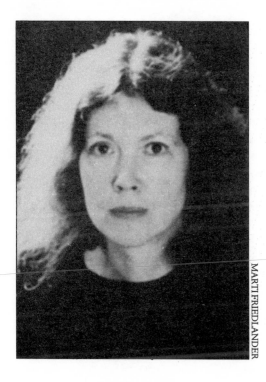

MARTI FRIEDLANDER

FLEUR ADCOCK

I never knew the early days of poetry at the Morden Tower: they were already in the glorious past when I did my first reading there, in 1977 (was it? And was that the time when I nearly missed the train from Carlisle to Newcastle, but the driver spotted me and brought the train back to the platform? He must have known I was going somewhere special.) Morden Tower readings were always special. When I lived in Newcastle, from 1979 to 1981, I went to plenty of them. I was at Basil Bunting's, sitting behind him on the windowsill – the floor was packed. Now that has gone into the glorious past. But glory continues; the one venue no poet will refuse is this one – along the dank, dark cobbled lane, up the rough stone steps, hoping the audience will find the place (most of them do). I look forward to the next twenty-five years.

FLEUR ADCOCK/*Nests*

Sniffing along the hedge for nests
where last year's thrushes were, I'm flapped at
from the sky: Whoosh! A wood-pigeon
trundles past to my neighbour's loft.

Not his pigeon-loft: the loft
where the water-tank is – access through
the gappy, slipping slates on his roof.
My neighbour's eccentric, you could say.

And so am I, and so am I;
but at least my garden's planted with flowers
and not, like his, with dead cats
and a wreath nicked from the cemetery.

No thrushes' nest this year, it seems.
They can't have liked it here, although
the wild-eyed prowlers are underground.
The pigeons have a cosier squat.

One of them's just about to exit:
my neighbour flings up what remains
of his bedroom window-frame: 'Out! Shoo!
Out!' He doesn't mind really.

– Or so I have to convince myself.
They mustn't mind, the mad and lonely,
being their unappealing selves;
we can't be doing with their emotions.

If he's so keen on pets, the pigeons
ought to console him. After all,
there was a time when he resented
inheriting all his sister's cats;

but then he fell for them. Lord, how long
did the last two lie in state, rotting
in his rotting house? And were they even
shrouded (please!) in plastic bags?

The wreath's as dead as a corn-dolly,
bleached to straw; but stuck in its frame
are half a dozen half-dead bluebells
and a sprig of, I suspect, my lilac.

GILLIAN ALLNUTT

I f you can negotiate the cobblestones of the alleyway
in fancy poetry-reading shoes and if you get there
early enough not to have to sit on a cloth-covered chair
(which will make you damp) and if you can remember
to remember the sixties with affection, it is very nice.

GILLIAN ALLNUTT/*Backyard*

Soul in the warm bean light
of the afternoon

be, without wings, a hanging-basket
or a water-butt

and pot-whole to the wild seed-hoard
that waits.

For the porcelain moon is broken into
shards,

the heart's
small skull-plates

open.

PETER ARMSTRONG

Initially, the Morden Tower was associated with childhood trips to St James's Park, when my father and I would make the detour by the then semi-derelict Blackfriars and the city wall. That must have been around the height of the Pickard/Bunting era, but little of that world was known to me until it surfaced as a rebel voice when Newcastle began to disintegrate under the plans of T. Dan Smith. Later, as an undergraduate, the true stature of Bunting came to my knowledge, and his was the first voice I heard at the Tower. My idea of the Tower is formed from these elements: something easily overlooked; something inclined to subversion; and something with a greater place in the wider cultural setting than we tend to realise. To this extent, the Tower takes its nature from the nature of the North East, and I'm glad to be part of that tradition.

PETER ARMSTRONG/Sunderland Nights

for Maurice Pierce, on hearing of his ordination

Brother,
      word has come, a grey decade after
our questionable mysteries, that you have put on black.
Pray for us, who, rat-arsed in high-ceilinged bars
dribbled metaphysics into our beer
and wanted women.
            Remember the stations we kept,
neon or the moon glancing off a wet road,
an east wind harassing
the sad provincial streets. God and alcohol:

I see you hunched over your smoke
and drink; 'Tonight I knelt in my room
and repented of my sins'; and me
yelling back across the swamped formica table
my crack-brained marriages of Paul and Sartre.

Let that be,
for now you come to mind I see us
stumbling to some outlying town
aimless circling speech having petered into silence
a quick-moving stranger gaining ground behind us.

PETER BENNET

*A*coustics are perfect and the atmosphere is unique.
I have never enjoyed hearing poetry more than in
the round stone room at the Morden Tower.

PETER BENNET/This Road, This Argument

Someone went through again last night
along this road, this argument.

How urgently
the slack hand on the wheel, the heavy foot,
ask to seem as though they meant it.

This is a dangerous route, not just a necklace
of lonely farms –
more like a cord as tight across a parcel
of moorland and plantation
as meaning ties action. And always, here,
because a small burn spent such ages
licking rock, we tumble to a narrow bridge
and error, maybe –
skid-marks and a little glass.

If death's the merest accident,
is life another? This road, this argument,
is after all predictable –
always the same trap, sudden, well-concealed,
that jerks the cord and lets the gut unravel.

MICHAEL BLACKBURN

I have had the good fortune to be for a short while a co-organiser at the Tower, as well as to have read there a number of times. Its physical shortcomings (up a dirty, ill-lit alley whose cobbles are covered with the refuse of Chinese restaurants; its lack of comforts – no toilet or taps, etc; and its frequent vandalising by drunks, druggies and vagrants) are more than made up for by its distinctively democratic and generous atmosphere. The Tower has had to resist the assault and neglect of vandals and philistines, and so, for me, if anything symbolises the true spirit of poetry in this country, it is the Morden Tower.

MICHAEL BLACKBURN/The Forgotten

Spreti, your face comes back to me
this autumn dawn, for no reason I can recall;
posthumous fame in the brevity of news,
you and your assassins, who saw the uniform
beneath the skin, that marked you as an enemy.

Still, this is the way of things;
news that is not news, while the trees
seal off their leaves and let them fall.

In a government office a typist cuts
her thumb on the edge of paper. She is
too young to remember your name, your face,
your fingers in a rigor about the broken
spectacles resting on your chest.

Leaves fall, numerous as memos.

There is no end to the freshness of victims.

PETE BROWN

I did the first reading, and also worked there with
Ginsberg, Bunting and Creeley, which I'm very proud
to have done, as well as many readings with Tom Pickard
and other talented natives. The thing I remember most
about it was the piano. The old piano was found dying
in the tower. When the audiences got bigger the piano
went outside on the wall. It then began falling apart,
aided by mischievous hands. Eventually it was distributed
along the walls and in the street, like mad sculptures
behind those pongy factories that used to vibrate through
the readings.

PETE BROWN/*House by the Airport*

Got a house by the airport
I watch the planes,
Their ebb and flow
When they come back to land
They fly so slow
Big tired birds
Still wired from their trip through time
Those angry eyes that stare through mist and snow
There are no words

Got a house by the airport
And there's a girl
Looks after me
When troubles come my way
She soothes my mind,
Long caring hands
Sharing me alongside all my ghosts
The wild songs they play still sound so fine
Hey listen man...

Got a house by the airport
In case the moment's ever ripe
When someone calls me up
And says, 'Come on,
We need you now
Old crazy head
Get blazing with your loaded axe,
Scare up some echoes, bring the sunburst down
And raise the dead...'

RICHARD CADDEL

The Morden Tower is quite simply the best poetry reading space I have experienced. I first came across it when I was a student, and in the early seventies I helped organise some of the readings. It was an unforgettable experience for me, and provided an opportunity to listen seriously to a wide range of writers: I'm still assimilating the lessons. I did my first serious public reading there – nobody could ask more than that in the way of luck.

RICHARD CADDEL/Three Foot Notes (yardstick)

footnote to Eric Mottram* Pierre Joris**
Ronald Johnson*** et al.

Antennae on their cabs
for antlers

each day my daughter
lured into their path

following the green man

   * A Book of Herne (Arrowspire Press, 1981)
  ** Antlers (New London Pride, 1975)
*** The Book of the Green Man (Longmans, 1967)

footnote to his own 'summer poems'
in time of elections again

The list of those who failed
would make a teasel wilt

I now realise
it is the Poet's Task
to rebuild the socialist movement

footnote
to a 'classic' book of southern poets

Littel boke
waur ye gannin

aw
jis doon thi 'library'

a gis

MATTHEW CALEY

The Morden Tower is simply unique. Its special atmosphere, presided over by that tiny, gargoyled angel near the roof-beams is the perfect setting to create proper interplay between audience and poet. And the audience is there to cheer, boo, cajole, ingest poetry rather than sit in the hushed reverence of the 'cultural event'. But the real highlight of reading at the tower is the opportunity, created by lack of toilet facilities, to further erode that sandstone groove in the alleyway wall, that has previously been worn down by such illustrious poetic forebears.

MATTHEW CALEY/Qwerty and the Hailstorm

Was barely knee-high
to his mother's only recently-seen knees
but would still step out boldly
with his head inside a Heinz-box
to feel the rattle of typewriter taps

pit the corrugations
blow by blow,
then back in, drenched, from the maelstrom
to watch the gift of one hailstone
delicately un-freeze
then melt to nothing in her Fairy-softened fist.

*

Now, with less precision,
his darting, one-fingered stabs
find H, then A, then I, then L,
but no drench comes beyond the one word 'hail'.

His head is yet again inside a Heinz-box,
cardboard from inside out,
and though he knows the story he must tell,
the blow by blow account

he can only wait and pray for the next hailstorm.

GEORGE CHARLTON

I have found the Tower's atmosphere can be weightier than air: a rosy cosiness or dank hostility depending on its mood and the weather's.

GEORGE CHARLTON/*The Widows at the Club*

It is all they have inherited from their late husbands –
Life membership to the workingmen's club
And a short-shrift to any outsider
Who inadvertently might have taken the place

Of one of them at the table they habitually sit at
On the same evening of each week – the only night out
Allowed them by their pensions
Which are otherwise so eaten into by things.

Their lipstick's cupid bows are askew
On slackened muscles and lines round their mouths,
The mingled raw scents of their perfumes taint
The taste of cherry brandies and substitute champagnes.

Always they seem just to have been missing
That one-last-number on the bingo card: when one or another
Collects a round from the bar, the jackpot is as far off as ever...
At the end of the evening's entertainment they will sing,

They will take a little longer than is usual
To check in their handbags for the key to the flat,
To find a cardigan or a glove. And outside, where one
Or two avenues of yellow streetlamps come together

They will take a little longer than most others
To make their goodbyes, to say 'Goodnight'...The flats
Are so small and awkwardly built, their coffins
Will end like their husbands' stuck in passageways.

TOMMY McCLEMENTS

BRENDAN CLEARY

I t's an honour and a privilege to have been associated with Morden Tower. Exciting and well-visited, it's a unique forum for live poetry. It has a ragged charm in these days of manifold disdain. What a shame *Arts Associations* are spending vast sums on glossy brochures advertising weekend schools in *Arts Management* or *Advertising and the Arts* or *The Arts and Private Sponsorship* when their funding and goodwill could be given to such a long-standing, honourable literary tradition as Morden Tower. Long may it prosper as the London poetry scene grinds to a halt in a stupor of safe middle-class complacent mediocrity.

BRENDAN CLEARY/*The Exchange Visit*

well i woke up this morning
& i was in Czechoslovakia
a peaceful suburb of Prague
to be exact

it had rained
so the lawns all glittered
& i had a splitting head
from too much 80% Vodka
well presumably so

the whole thing is a mystery
because now i talk the language
i have a Czech wife
three handsome healthy Czech children
(for the moment their names escape me)
a Czech house with a Czech roof
overlooking a Czech swimming pool

what luxury!

it's really quite some existence
i've had carved out for myself
& i've read Kafka in the original
& all my old favourites like Philip Marlowe
in handy pocket-size Czech translations

still i have a job remembering
how i fell asleep
beneath the shadow
of the lame cow
at the edge of Mulligan's field
in the drizzle
in the breezes whirling tractor blades
in the old sod

yes i have a job recollecting
how i woke like this hungover
in this suburb of Prague
which thankfully is very handy
to all of the shops

what utter luxury…

BOB COBBING

M orden Tower – simply the most congenial place
in the world in which to perform poetry.

BOB COBBING/*Square Poem*

This   is   a   square   poem.
This   poem   is   a   square.
Is   this   square   a   poem?
This   square   is   a   poem.
This   square   is.   A   poem
Is   a   poem   –   this   square.
This   is   a   poem-square.
A   poem-square   is   this
Poem.   This   is   a   square.
A   square   poem   is   this
Square.   This   is   a   poem,
This   is.   A   poem-square.

DAVE FARRANTS

TONY CURTIS

I remember the warm reception the Tower gave me in '87 and the special sense of all our illustrious predecessors as readers.

TONY CURTIS/*Caitlin Macnamara*

He sees a gypsy princess, seventeen,
head proudly high and turned to the future
– that would be Dylan and children,
the loving fights at Laugharne and the ocean flight
to her marble cherub slabbed in Manhattan.

But here it is still rose-bloom, tumbling hair,
neck like a waterfall crashing in the light
to firm breasts Augustus John
eyed until it hurt, neglecting the detail
of hands on hips, the folds of her skirt.

She flames with a young woman's fire
and he, mid-life, the blaze of his beard
and hair dimming, would lead her
to Dylan, paint *the happy schoolboy* and later
punch him flat with jealousy on the Carmarthen road.

He sees her glow and swell with her womanhood
set there on a reclaimed canvas so that hidden
in her womb she has the inverted head
of an abandoned sitter, a dark-haired woman
who stares. A ghost patterned in the pullover

that he would rise to adjust,
and in adjusting open, remove
and let fall to the studio floor.
What is it this painting loves?
Youth, breasts, hair – the persistent ghost?

And did she, seeing it finished,
feel the user or the used?
Whatever feelings the paint fixed that day
are held half a life, half a legend away.
Museum piece, catalogue note, truth and art confused.

IVOR CUTLER

My strongest memory is of the cold. And the shock of seeing a queue all the way from the pub to the front door of the Morden Tower waiting patiently in the sub-zero temperature to hear poetry. All those chilled bladders!

IVOR CUTLER/Timothy

He planted his window boxes
with perennial rye, cocksfoot
& Timothy, stood a clay sheep
& a clay cow in each, carefully
wrote down his conclusions,
then sent a letter to
'Farmer's Weekly' which has
since become famous.

CAROL ANN DUFFY

Although I had a lovely time in Newcastle, the audience, as I recall, was very small!

CAROL ANN DUFFY/*Hard To Say*

I asked him to give me an image for Love, something I could see,
or imagine seeing, or something that, because of the word
for its smell, would make me remember, something possible
to hear. *Don't just say love*, I said, *love, love, I love you.*

On the way home, I thought of our love and how, lately,
I too have grown lazy in expressing it, snuggling up to you
in bed, idly murmuring those tired clichés without even thinking.
My words have been grubby confetti, faded, tacky, blown far

from the wedding feast. And so it was, with a sudden shock of love,
like a peacock flashing wide its hundred eyes, or a boy's voice
flinging top G to the roof of an empty church, or a bottle
of French perfume knocked off the shelf, spilling into the steamy bath,

I wanted you. After the wine, the flowers I brought you drowned
in the darkening light. As we slept, we breathed their scent all night.

HELEN DUNMORE

I read at Morden Tower in May 1983, with Carol Rumens. My first collection of poems, 'The Apple Fall', was launched by Bloodaxe at this reading. I remember a mixture of delight, tension and shyness. At last I had a book in my hands which summed up seven years' work, and I was able to read from it among people who showed generous warmth and interest. I liked the shape of the Tower. Its roundness and oldness broke down barriers between reader and audience. We were drawn together around the focus of the poetry. A man kept taking photographs, and later he sent me some of them. Nearly seven more years have passed, and the person in the photographs looks young to me now, with her new book in her hands. But the Tower is still the same, I hope.

HELEN DUNMORE/Rinsing

In the corded hollows of the wood
leaves fall.
How light it is.
The trees are rinsing themselves of leaves
like Degas laundresses, their forearms
cold with the jelly-smooth
blue of starch-water.

The laundresses lean back and yawn
with their arms still in the water
like beech-boughs, pliant
on leavings of air.

In the corded hollows of the wood
how light it is.
How my excitement
burns in the chamber.

PAUL DURCAN

I felt very privileged to be reading at the Morden Tower. The very name is resonant of things ultimate, holy, profane, sacred, humble, stark. For twenty years or more I've carried the name in my head, associating it with Tyneside, Northumbria, Bob Davenport, Basil Bunting, Tom Pickard – singers and poets I deeply respect and admire.

PAUL DURCAN/The Odd Little White Breast

A small black woman
Who is a divorcee
Is consecrated
A bishop in Boston.

Will it be long now
Until a small black woman
Who is a divorcee
Will be consecrated
A bishop in Ireland?

For in Ireland also
Not all of God's children
Have got penises.
Around the Cliffs of Moher
The odd breast has been spotted,
The odd little white breast.

ALISTAIR ELLIOT

P oetry doesn't seem a wet occupation at the Tower.
I suppose it's the broken glass, piss and vomit on
the cobbles, or the vague memory of stone cannonballs
directed at the Town Wall. I go out of my way to walk
by there.

ALISTAIR ELLIOT/*Old Bewick*

We come for a day of peace: the wick
of bees, the ripples widening on a rock
scratched by fingers that never fondled iron,
the lumpy mattress of moor, with cairns for buttons,
the curves of Cheviot and marine horizons.

We learn the place was given as a reward
to a Northumbrian who killed Malcolm the Third,
Macbeth's successor: crime and death
to delight, instruct and move. We thread the gate
on to the common, dazed by northern heat.

A mile to Blawearie. Something quicker than time
and rain has broken the grey abandoned farm:
somebody has been practising war. We eat
in sycamore shade, staying under cover
when a helicopter rises and slides over.

Three fleas hang on the skyline, trailing ropes
or legs or smoke. They hide and hop
over our heads, scattering turds of sound.
The curlews have to cry a little louder
to keep a territory on the Border.

For this is still the Debatable Land. In cities,
in rooms, you can forget the competition.
Here in the heather, when our earth lies open
and the sun takes it, you feel the very ground
of fighting, the fatal impulse to defend.

ROY FISHER

The Morden Tower's in a different country from most other places where poetry's read: it's better. I first came to it on a winter Saturday early in 1965 or 1966. Tom Pickard met me, a well-grown youth in yellow boots, with a face under his hair; marvellously friendly, optimistic and embattled, and swearing terribly. At the Pickards' flat in Jesmond, Basil Bunting was sitting by the fire with a mug of tea and a notebook, finishing 'What the Chairman Told Tom', which he'd been writing on the train from Wylam; later, in the sagging throne of an arm-chair by the smoky fire in the Tower, he gave it its first reading. I was an uneasy reader in those days, and most of the poetry I had to read was such sour stuff that it depressed even me; but the palpable receptivity for poetry leaned back against what I'd brought, and held it up. I've never read at the Tower without learning something.

Strong juices, smokes inhaled,
forced hyperventilations, drum-noise
peel back the shaman's brain and leave
clear passage for the gods to speak,
rasping and limited and low,
with magic voices they make up
in the hollow of his fled
human voice.

       For years, the two
elect rulers of the English West
have also been divine. They've both been
out to the market and bought
special strange voices for telling us
special strange things, which no normal person
could utter. It's
what the people expect.

ALLEN GINSBERG

A crowded evening, candles, incense, music, beautiful-bodied company, stone walls, Pickard with the haircut of a valiant magician's attendant in charge of the Tower's rare library, Bunting the master himself smiling on the fête – so I gave the most complete reading of my own written work that I ever vocalised in one evening. Knowing the minds and ears were fine (or among the younger folk, if inexperienced, tenderly open), I began at my beginning as a poet and read past midnight all the scribing I had done for a decade. Certainly happy circumstances for a poet, and happier to hear Bunting's concern – 'Too many words, condense still more'. Thus the reading at Morden Tower altered my own poetic practice slightly toward greater economy of presentation. So I learned more reading at Morden Tower than I had at a hundred universities.

ALLEN GINSBERG/*What the Sea Throws Up At Vlissengen*

for Simon Vinkenoog

Plastic & cellophane, milk cartons & yogurt containers blue & orange
    shopping bag nets
Clementine peels, papersacks, feathers & kelp, bricks & sticks,
succulent green leaves & pine tips, waterbottles, plywood and tobacco
    pouches
Coffee jartops, milkbottle caps, rice bags, blue rope, an old brown
    shoe, an onion skin
Concrete chunks white pebbled, sea biscuits, detergent squeezers,
    bark and boards, a whisk-brush, a box top
Formula A Dismantling Spray-can, a whole small brown onion, a
    yellow cup
A boy with two canes walking the shore, a dead gull, a blue running
    shoe,
a shopping bag handle, lemon half, celery bunch, a cloth net –
Cork bottletop, grapefruit, rubber glove, wet firework tubes,
masses of iron-brown-tinted seaweed along the high water mark near
    the sea wall
a plastic car fender, green helmet broken in half, giant hemp rope
    knot, tree trunk stripped of bark,
a wooden stake, a bucket, myriad plastic bottles, pasta Zara pack,
a long grey plastic oildrum, bandage roll, glass bottle, tin can, Christmas
    pine tree
a rusty iron pipe, me and my peepee.

1/3/83

LEE HARWOOD

I've read a number of times at the Tower over the last twenty years, especially in the 1960s and early 70s, and it's always been a pleasure. A place to read where people actually listen and are well read in contemporary poetry. No need for explanations, you just present your work and know it will be heard. Such energy and warmth in an audience are rare.

LEE HARWOOD/*Torpedoed Yet Again*

on a clear spring night…
                              …the aging ship goes down,
roars and sighs, then slides almost silently under the waves.
Clinging desperately to the fragments of wreckage,
avoiding a lung-full of oil, avoiding the flaming fuel,
I clumsily splash through the dark waters
blindly clasping what I don't even know.

A new moon rises early in the evening
over the mountain valley
– that's too many miles away –
silhouetting the forest on the ridge
and the now ghostly snow-patched peak beyond.

That's all ashore. And where does that leave me?
tied obsessively to a past that *is* right
but comes hard to match with present circumstances.
No? No, that's not how to put it.
Right to believe in that 'magic', that love?

And so – here we are again – I can't see you
but know you're somewhere there in the darkness.
Not splashing sounds but like a presence.
The mermaids though are off-duty tonight.

You're here again and I'm here again
in my dream at least,
though your body moves purposefully
a long way away from this watery site.

I'd gladly put you on a pedestal but don't
as I value you more than those empty obsessions.
We're not perfect beasts, I know.

I pray I bump into a rubber raft soon.

GEOFF HATTERSLEY

I first read at the Morden Tower in February 1987. It was a good night, though my memory of it is very much tied in with meeting Brendan Cleary. He had just published my first pamphlet, 'The Deep End', and it was good to be able to put a face to him. The reading itself went extremely well – I consider it one of the two most enjoyable I've done.

GEOFF HATTERSLEY/Columbo Is Hamlet

It's not a generous cunninlingus
we can hear, just the cat washing herself.
It's the best thing I've said all night. We both
felt so dull-stupid from work, watched Magnum

and MASH: The first and second signs. Beside
Magnum, Columbo is Hamlet. Our legs
entwined, we're talking now of tomorrow,
planning for it: The garden. The second

coat of paint in the kitchen. The bloody
washing and shopping. A drink or seven.
You need to go places, meet people, touch.
You need to stop feeling so tired. Mostly

you need to know when I'll reach into my
jeans pocket, come out with something other
than dirty handkerchiefs, bent paper clips,
and nothing. You could have a point. The cat

is quiet now, as people drift home from
the pubs, slamming doors and shouting. Across
the road we hear their slight concerns: New ways
to take, and jobs for good money, not love.

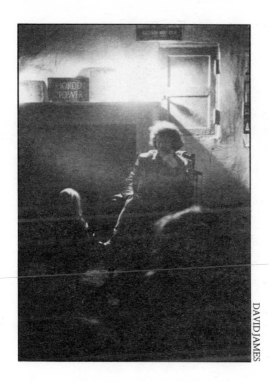

SEAMUS HEANEY

Morden Tower is one of the best places in the world for a poetry reading – especially if there is an electricity strike. The power was off when I visited in 1972, and the cold stone and candle flames gave the occasion an unforgettable glamour. And who's to say whether it was the fumes from the hot wax or the intensity of homesickness that caused another Irish poet in the audience that night to pass out? May the opportunities for being overcome in the Tower continue to prevail for another twenty-five years.

SEAMUS HEANEY/Three Rich Hours

for Benedict Kiely

1.

One afternoon I was seraph on gold leaf.
I stood on the railway sleepers, hearing larks,
Grasshoppers, cuckoos, dogbarks, trainer planes

Cutting and modulating and drawing off.
Heat wavered on the immaculate line
And shine of the cogged rails. On either side,

Dog daisies stood like vestals, the hot stones
Were clover-meshed and streaked with engine oil.
Air spanned, passage waited, the balance rode,

Nothing prevailed, everything divined
What was in store already taking place
In a time marked by assent and by hiatus.

2.

And strike this scene in gold too, in relief,
So that a greedy eye cannot exhaust it:
Stable straw, Rembrandt-gleam and burnish

Where my father bends to a tea-chest packed with salt,
The hurricane lamp held up at eye-level
In his bunched left fist, his right hand foraging

For the unbleeding, vivid-fleshed bacon,
Home-cured hocks pulled up into the light
For pondering a while and putting back.

That night I owned the piled grain of Egypt.
I watched the sentry's torchlight on the hoard.
I stood in the door, unseen and blazed upon.

3.

Rat poison the colour of blood pudding
Went phosphorescent when it was being spread:
Its sparky rancid shine under the blade

Brought everything to life – like news of murder
Or the charge of a parked car occupied by lovers
On a side road, or stories of bull victims.

If a muse had sung the anger of Achilles
It could not have heightened the world-danger more.
It was all there in the fresh rat poison,

Corposant on mouldy, dried-up crusts.
On winter evenings I loved its reek and risk.
And windfalls freezing on the outhouse roof.

DAVID JAMES

LIBBY HOUSTON

I had heard a great deal about the Morden Tower, about Tom Pickard and Basil Bunting and the poetry renaissance in Newcastle before I came here in the 60s, and I was really pleased to be invited back in 1983 and 1989. I guess it represents for me what was best about the Beat movement – the breaking down of social barriers both of class and education; the release of poetry from a restrictive literariness and the equation of a long face, or dry obscurity, with profundity; and an enjoyment of the richness of language including spoken language, and of the music of speech. I don't know what it's taken to keep the place going, nor who has made sure that it has kept going. But I want to say thank you. This anniversary is a triumph, and probably hard-won.

LIBBY HOUSTON/*Stanage, Going South*

One in green rich as holly on the watery white
and one whose harsh orange the mist has turned radiant,

friends that I follow, heading for the cloud on High Neb
at a pace harried by the wind as it bursts up the edge –

Off on the left a sheep bleats once or twice peevishly.
A grouse blows past. The trees are held down. Alone

I would still have had the blond grass glow, true, and the scud.
But the two I shadowed gave the landscape figures

and colour, colour the dark white intensified
and the figures scale, yes, as they would in a photo

or painting – those pointing groups on mountains; but now too
a mirror of the intricate steps quick judgments the delight

called up by fast going on uneven ground across wind
like this. Also I could know the cold I felt was shared.

TONY JACKSON

B etween 1964 when I was just a brief boy of only
19 when Tom & Connie first opened the doors
for Ginsberg Nuttall Hollo Corso Bly et al and today
this year quarter of a century later

        we all grew up/YUK
got old high got sad lost youth fell in love many times
got addicted to various stuff cleaned-up even stops smok-
ing but as divine Stein would have said had she been
around poetry under any name is equal junk or even
ice-cream

    while some shot-up others injected Black
Mountain and to o.d. on either had much the same
effect we're told.
And now years later with a number gone & some dead
& others not even able to walk or climb stone stairs up
into the tower

      we all still remember days of open explore
& tremble excitement that is how it was how those days
before many of us still remember.

TONY JACKSON/*Painted Walls*

Come forth sweet night & bring long lines
of silver sackbuts
Turn velvet nobs aside for Orlando Gibbons
is at the door
Sleeves slashed to display under-arm burn
of tender scarlet
      and ankles twist to resemble those
of a tiny ballet dancer
And if I were to produce a piece
              of sudden sound
call it music if you really must
           it would be more
a slice of silence than anything you or I
have ever known before
Grim Orlando stands before us
          his hands across
our eyes like a brutal blindfold to close
us down / shut out with silence
Tra-la Tra-la
Tra-la Tra-la
Mrs Gibbons' wee boy glimmers
           Burnished smoke
streams from between his wonderous thighs

RICHARD KELL

One of the admirable qualities of the Tower has been its wide-ranging hospitality. To have accommodated for 25 years such variety of subject-matter, style (in reading as well as writing), age, nationality, and reputation – while maintaining a high poetic standard – is a contribution to liberal culture which deserves our gratitude.

RICHARD KELL/*At the Summit*

Campi Flegeiri? Vesuvius? You preferred
the catacombs of Rome.
I understand; but graves and reeking vents
give you the full circle,
whose continuity then elides
both endings and beginnings.

That labyrinth was man-made, yes,
but formed, like the convoluted brain,
the small green lizards flicking
on slopes of tuff, the broom
flowering where ashes fell,
by constant replication.

It's disappointing, after the slow climb,
to find the crater dry as death,
filled with volcanic debris:
no pouting mud or sighing fumarole
hints at the awesome fires
of genesis, growth, survival.

But think how close we are
to turbulence, and so
to a strange order, something we couldn't see
though the pit boiled and flared:
graces and infinite repetitions
no maze of tombs can equal.

AUGUST KLEINZAHLER

There have always been three places I wanted to read my poetry: St Mark's Church in the Bowery (NYC), Morden Tower, and a private college for girls in Copenhagen, almost any of them. Having known and studied with Basil Bunting it was a particular thrill to read at the Tower and piss at the foot of it, which, as the worn stone attests, has been well-watered over the centuries. My one regret is that I haven't lived close enough by to enjoy Tower readings through the years. The Tower is a magical place and we have nothing in the States quite so special. Don't let Thatcher find out about it, I beg of you. Hail Tom and Connie Pickard and all their noble successors in keeping the series alive.

AUGUST KLEINZAHLER/Friends Through at New Year's

The old year's calendars flutter down
in the mist,
            countless sheets
of dated memoranda escorting them like pilot fish
to the street below

as friends pass through, alone and with kids:
the one down from Juneau
headed south to Belize for the diving;
and the clan from Vancouver, two little girls now
and a grubstake to buy a boat with, sail
the islands off of Crete, Turkey maybe, just way
the hell away from housepainting and rain.

We watch cartoons as front after front
sweeps through,
                worse than Vancouver. – This is worse
than Vancouver, she says,
but they all go to the carrousel in the park anyhow
and catch cold
because the big one remembers from last time.

The other friend is drinking, talking
about the woman back up in Sitka, how the last letter
was strange;
                and her youngest boy, Tom,
the way the two of them got along.

When old friends speak of the past
after the years apart, lives so different,
                                how well
they seem to know us, still,
after such a long time, better than our families,
our lovers.
                      So much of ourselves that we had forgotten
alive in them still

whose children fall asleep in our arms.

TOM LEONARD

M orden Tower *will always have Sixties associations
for me as a place I knew about though never
visited when I was first discovering Creeley, Zukofsky,
Olson, Robbe-Grillet, and all the Grove and Calderbook
authors. It was a kind of legendary place obviously run
and frequented by people who cared about the same type
of writing as I did – or were at least against the same type.*

*I've read twice there since 1984. Both times I had
the sense of going from the pub where I'd met the organis-
ers up a lane to a place opened up specially for the
evening's purpose, with calor gas fires blazing away to
fight what was real winter cold. The poem 'at a poetry
reading' here does not refer to a Morden Tower reading.*

TOM LEONARD/*at a poetry reading*

he wears his profundity on his sleeve;
he was the man, he suffered –
he was there:

and now, I am here
and you are there
and you are there very much
in your own sense of presence

at being here
and I am beginning to suffer
at your being here too
instead of there.

oh I wish you were back there
I'm sorry it's rotten but
I wish you were back there
and I was still here

alone with the potted plants
and the polite audience
and Life which is a hoot
it's fandabbydozy

and it's been like that
since they first held me upside down
and I started roaring
with laughter

oh bad faith bad faith
cried surgeon magee
but me dear old mammy
whispered softly to me

authenticity will out
with or without
a smile on its face

LIZ LOCHHEAD

Morden Tower is the most exciting place I have ever read poems. People cram in and hug around you, perching on stone ledges as the chairs run out. One or two people only have provided themselves with a nip of whisky, as I do, warming my voice before reading. With the audience in their big tweed coats and their cheeks still glowing from the cold cobbles they've clattered along, past Chinese restaurant smells of star anise and five-season powder, soon we won't need the reeking calor gas fires any more. In these old walls you can whisper and still be heard, or ring out loud as you like, ringed around with laughter, and a special sort of attention that breathes in unison, giving out before they take in, and giving out again.

LIZ LOCHHEAD/In the museum of anthropology I consider the similarity between the art of the 'tupalik' and the writing of a poem

What is it?

It is imaginary, magically created.
It is often grotesque.
It is part human, part animal, part sea creature.
It has a bloated belly and its teeth are bared,
It is domestic as dirty dishes,
as ordinary as terror.
Among the Inuit,
where coca cola has rotted the milkteeth of
all the children,
such graven images are often no bigger
than the little finger.

NORMAN MacCAIG

I've read there twice (if not three times) and have fond memories of all of them, firstly because of the unique nature of the place, but more importantly because of the friendly and responsive audiences – not to mention the organisers. I forget many places where I've given readings, but not the Morden Tower.

NORMAN MacCAIG/London to Edinburgh

I'm waiting for the moment
when the train crosses the Border
and home creeps closer
at seventy miles an hour.

I dismiss the last two days
and their friendly strangers
into the past
that grows bigger every minute.

The train sounds urgent as I am,
it says home and home and home.
I light a cigarette
and sit smiling in the corner.

Scotland, I rush towards you
into my future that,
every minute,
grows smaller and smaller.

IAN McMILLAN

Being a stand-up poet is a silly job, and it involves you performing in all sorts of venues in front of all kinds of people, and it's good to have some kind of ideal in the back of the head in those gloomy rooms. The ideal I carry is the Morden Tower: I've only read there once, and I enjoyed it very much, but in an era where venues come and go it represents continuity and commitment in a changing world. Long may it continue, then I can have it in my head as I perform to the organiser and a caretaker in a dusty room in an FE college suffering terminal cuts.

IAN MCMILLAN/Song for Roof Building (collected in South Yorkshire Light Industry Park, Barnsley)

*to be accompanied
by traditional
hammering with
roof-building tools*

Say a man has three shillings.
Would you tell me, would you tell me
who the man is with the three shillings?

Build part of the roof!

I know he is not me.
It is not me with the three shillings.
Not me with the three bob.

Build part of the roof!

I have seen them, the men
without three shillings
in this land with no poverty.

Build part of the roof!

I have seen them rubbing
their legs together
to keep warm, to make light.

Build part of the roof!

But this is only a song, after all,
to help me build this roof.
I do not care about the three shilling.

Build part of the roof!

Say a man has three shillings.
Would you tell me, would you tell me
who the man is with the three shillings?

Build part of the roof!

BARRY MacSWEENEY

I was 15, still at school, and burning with a desire to write, seriously and well. Amazingly, Rutherford Grammar School had the City Lights edition of Ginsberg's 'Howl' in its library. You might imagine the effect that had on a lad raised on Wordsworth. Only weeks later that summer Ginsberg came to England for the Albert Hall reading – and visited the Tower. It was a packed, brilliant evening. After his visit, visitors to the Tower included, in quick succession, Corso, Ferlinghetti, Dorn, Creeley, Trocchi, Harwood, Raworth, many of the younger British poets, writers from all over the world – and, of course, Bunting. Week after week, the living word! What better introduction to writing could a young poet have had?

BARRY MacSWEENEY/Ode

COMPLETELY FRAGGED IN THIS NEW DAWN
    with the stainless bint in No.10
      a nation aches for harmony:
   population culled Northumberland to Kent, as if
   a shrike at large
                      beyond the normal row. Time
    and small returns, bloodmoney on the road
    now the banner's down. Hotspur's done
 his foolish marching
       and the pasture's cold, all traces
         rinsed to roots. Bede is with him
        in the sorry ground.

O many lost
       & harmful
              to a sudden core –
nothing
    like it
       under heaven.

Such confidence when the applause is blue!
      For we are harried from docks and mines
     to the very close, striking off
 as best can. To fend too hard
    will dent your hands, dear one,
 which I would not wish.

Now the complete ordinance
     weeps & moans
& the beautiful newsreader
     repeats each
tremendous fairytale.

GORDON BROWN

WILLIAM MARTIN

First came to the Tower some time in the sixties to hear Adrian Mitchell. Thought it was one of the towers down by the river, so the second half was well under way when I got there. Just managed to squeeze in by the door. Coming to the Tower nowadays up the now lit, narrow back lane, between Stowell Street and the Wall, the temptations of stale exotic smells from the extractor fans of the many Chinese restaurants, have to be resisted first. It is usually worth it. The Tower is not noted for its decoration, except for the moulded plaster angel and the Tree of Life high up on the walls, but the tradition of spoken poetry, 'like a seamless garment o' music and thought' lives on, and is vigorous and varied as it should be.

WILLIAM MARTIN/*Where Is Our Feeding*

1.

Uncounted crownings
Sighted like starlings

July migration unperched
By her caller's knock

Silver prize bandsmen warm
Breath-horns in gathering

Winged noise grows louder
Till seven strikes down-wind

Silk banner flappings they'll follow

2.

Here and here our Jerusalem
Is under this sun crowded

Not under unconscious collective
But all things in open bright day

Bairns touch banner hem
For power proudly winded

Our banner played
Down town-road redeemed
To candymen lost

3.

Fellside-bread brought once
To make words here

Crust-syllables syntax
Real eating for every day

Water table drinking springs
Mark scoffed lines
This noontide laid out

(Not special Sabbath words
Rumbling hungry indoors)

All tasted and shared

4.

Where is our feeding to come

The banners say know who you are
And know you must stand together

Will it come out of sky
Sun clouded with bird flight

Will it spout from the sea's edge
Shoals secretly gasping

Where is our feeding
To Tom Dick and Harry

The banners say know who you are

ADRIAN MITCHELL

When I first read at the Morden Tower the floor was jampacked with people. There was no electricity so a lad was stationed by me holding a candle which dripped red wax over my poems as we went along. I came back whenever I could. It was about the best audience in England, not the biggest, but the warmest and the most intent. I remember the Tower and my guardian angels, Tom and Connie Pickard, with incredulous affection.

ADRIAN MITCHELL/The Murder of the Poet Michael Smith by Three Men in Kingston, Jamaica

      You!
You don't belong here.
Why are you walking here?

      You!
You don't belong here.
Why are you walking here?

      You!
You don't belong here.
Why are you walking here?

               I am a free man.
            I walk anywhere in this land.

GERALDINE MONK

Newcastle has a tower echoing with poetry. This is not a poetic image; it is a reality. It is poetry live and alive; poetry without apology. Flourish on!

GERALDINE MONK/*A Eulogy Written in an Unmarked Northern City Pub*

It is night. Or. It is day. It is timeless.
Sporadic fighting breaks. Is quickly quelled.
All things considered. Proximity excites. Generating passion.
Desirability. To have contact. To consume. To drink deep.
Long. Soft. Hard. Break and.
Soak.
Bread.

Green light from shaded pool. Tables of time without tide.
The lilt of tower blocks with awakenings in the sky or
hibernations entrenched in basement undergrowths.
Rarely at street level. Few wise. Most nibble and peck.
Nuts.
Seeds.

It is see-saw-jig-saw.
     Endless pieces. Parties of choice. And much.
     Wet squelching litter. Concrete. Jolly kiss o' life.
     Painted paddock. Balls. Bells. Tail backs. Feathers.
     Dashes. Exhausts. Upside. Turnaround. Roundabout.
Let's take away.
Buttercross.
Hot fried fishes.

It is still night. It is still day. It is moving. Timeless.
The traffic.
The cues.
The ebb and flow and chink of glasses.
The spills.
The queues.

All jam. All runny.
Cherry Cake.

VINCE MORRISON

My recollections of the hallowed walls are coloured (amber) by ebriosity mostly. However, I enjoyed the 1986 Festival of Peace reading when twelve hours of a Saturday were devoted to continuous gurglings, bellowings (myself) and eructative intonations. The steps and alleyway leading to the Tower resembled a cross between the January sales and the second round of the Simod cup (Dante Alighieri 5, München Heine 3; match abandoned after assorted spondees and rondeaux were found in the Kraut's goalmouth!)

VINCE MORRISON/*Close*

for Karen Lammers

Before the cloudburst, Phantoms overhead
rousing strays from a tin coop.
'In the mood' stirs a Yopster opposite.
Sweating with hoes and gripe
his silver blades like fins
skive through polyanths, chickweed alike.
The gaffer damns Christ and spinach
both are turning to seed.

While lion's teeth digest our 'lawn'
plastic sacks of last year's cuttings
shimmer like seals.
She squats on a burst settee,
goose-skin stippling her scorched forearms;
translating sigh for sigh, Heaney's 'Casualty'.
Unlike on vicious shrubs that encroach her borders,
no ginger drones cling to blossoms on slow water.
Someone walks over her grave.

ERIC MOTTRAM

*A*sked a couple of times to read at Morden Tower in the 1960s became an honour – considering the distinguished poets from Britain and abroad that read there. A sort of accolade. When I returned to take part in the Bunting film made by Tyne Tees TV, just walking down the cobbled lane and up the steep steps to the room vividly recalled those tremendous days. The Pickards had established Morden Tower as a centre of poetry reading with an international reputation – and at a time in Britain when poetry readings were entirely rare. You could be sure of an alert knowledgeable audience, sitting near enough to be spoken to rather than addressed. The circular room afforded that character of intimacy. Even the occasional smoke gusting from the ancient chimney added particularity!

ERIC MOTTRAM/For Basil Bunting (2)

trees do not tear the sky
constellations do not rise

the prodigal old man is
telling his life story

day after day is not 6 810 000 litres
per second Niagara simplicity

was it he grasped my hand
at the main road who did in Buffalo

we gaze at the Hermitage hear
a curlew in this grey windsweep

again in upland mist round Bewcastle
cross life tree twines in runes

north between
Vikings and Celts

it is given to some men to discover
their world in the world

in endless stories they listen in
shed what is known

a decent contempt above
trained snouting for truffles

air takes any body vanishes
a long arduous trek the path ice

through equilibrium contests
boxed restless particles

a journey song weaves times
designs how love conjugates a land

to divisions score partition
a cadence discovers lies ahead

entering a land new to tread caress
sounds to be located time and distance

in cotton grass and Sourgill Force
what near is and far a horizon under hand

a string and paper job lands on Town Moor
in a boy's game explosions but it is a plane

the old man's mocking laughs
at destruction just escaped

the route lay through prisons
in a century's variety

subterranean pleasures in hiding
under the nations' intelligence

some mentally ill feel no pain
stricken and look through a paneless frame

but cannot sit in a high room
high ceiling distances through light

quiet without rest or restlessness
his forms a song to be sung again

as their music claims refusals
but directs towards nodes you

may receive fire from
may die may sing from

in one world burrowing another stand
emerge on a Dent peak beard taut to dale wind

HENRY NORMAL

There's a theory that emotion is imprinted on walls like music on vinyl. If this is so, the walls of the Morden Tower must bear one of the most beautiful symphonies of passion and life.

HENRY NORMAL/*A More Intimate Fame*

She licked the applause from the fingers of each hand
       like honey drips from toast
but could never hold on tight enough
    to that for which she hungered most
Only let into the heart like a holiday home
      though always a paying guest
scratching for dignity from blind hope
      but knowing dignity is still second best
Love has always been one of those rooms at parties
     that she'd never dare venture inside
where close friends sat crosslegged on floorboards
      and she had no invite
Always outstretched arms at railway stations
      into which she'd never run
or couples on buses in matching jumpers unashamed to
         dress as one
This time though she thought she'd sneaked unnoticed into the
    gates of Heaven – Accepted for her sins
but she clung too tight never understanding
     how fragile a thing are wings
and when the regret welled up inside
there was no cradle for her soul and her broken pride
how can it hurt so much if the love has died?
and soon all the narrow eyes and shallow lives
      became a noose around her neck
until accelerating into fog the drink cocooned her head
how can you love so much
how can you love so much
how can you love so much and have nothing left

JEFF NUTTALL

Newcastle wasn't just the best audience for poetry in the sixties and seventies, it was the only truly appreciative one. London audiences were small and clique-ish, largely devoted to the non-poetry of the Movement and its aftermath. Liverpool audiences were trendy and music orientated. But the Newcastle audiences listened, understood and actually applauded the points in a poem when the poet knew something had been achieved. I remember the Tower as being a place you had to warm yourself on the architecture, the sense of being studded into a medieval wall, because there were damn few creature comforts beyond that, not even the usual sanitary offices. I learned how to negotiate a spiked fence along the wall. I don't know what everybody else did.

JEFF NUTTALL/untitled

So brightly blisters the great regurgitating ribbon
                    of the Thames.
Sculls skim through like springtime swallows.
Keels kiss tidal scum, lancing the stolen sun-boils.

Echoes of these peppery explosions
Paint the ceiling of the Depot Wine Bar & Bistro
In a dancing manner of a watering,
Watering this way and watering that.

The Jab Bug can be heard from a distance,
Her twittering, her nesting-season-screams,
Her word-stabs.

The Jab Bug is so small and so appealing –
Her dawning innocence inciting hen-squawks.
The Jab Bug's cunt is not always as the running river of goodness.
                    Just usually.

The glistening ribbon bends about the same way,
On the same elephantine curve.
The popping pods of spat light
Dither across the ceiling of the Depot Wine Bar & Bistro
And what the hell can a heart do
Yearning towards the blacker plums of love
But munch on the peanuts, the unusually shaped potato crisps.

MOIRA CONWAY

SEAN O'BRIEN

I think of Morden Tower as a congenial aerial dungeon which I can never find by myself. The damp and the state of decoration serve as reminders that the audience for poetry is a serious one: no ballgowns and dinner jackets here, and perhaps no heating either. Long may the place and the people flourish.

SEAN O'BRIEN/*At the Wellgate*

Their speechless cries left hanging in the cold
As human fog, as auditory stench,
The boreal flâneurs donate their stains
And thick cirrhotic sherries to the bench
Outside the precinct where they're not allowed,
And finding they've no stories left to tell
And thus no purchase on the Christmas crowd,
Descend by means of manholes into Hell.

Which in their case is Arctic and unmapped,
Its every inch the coiling thick of it,
As if the Piranesi of the tubes
Had framed a labyrinth of frozen shit,
In which they wander howling and rehearse
The notion that elsewhere could still be worse.

TOM PICKARD

F or a time, during the sixties, it was a very exciting place to be. It broke down class barriers in a joyful mix of marijuana, alcohol, neat poetry and music.

TOM PICKARD/*what maks makems*

an icy wind bites
    through stocks
whipped-up
           from the Wear
  where shags in a frozen
  dive
break black water

    a crick-necked welder
bent
    beneath the boat
with his head in a screen
    – flash on her
un-named belly –
    burning her together
section by section

    he crawls
in an eighteen inch
    double bottom
beneath the engine room
  tank-top
to the sump
  where the clatter
    and rattle of caulkers
shatter the ear
  drum running shudder
of a bulkhead drop

the only way out
in a panic
is backwards
over
    an extractor pipe
and cables
  through a hatch
    got smaller
in a swollen flap

the Makem can
  weld himself into
      a steel coffin
and seal the lid on
      afterwards

J.H. PRYNNE

The Tower was a great hub of activity in the early years. Now on a recent visit to the city I see that smart civic improvement is creeping about like a fungus; but the street along by the Tower is unscathed, 'without a counterpart' as Browning says.

J.H. PRYNNE/Fool's Bracelet

In the day park shared by advancement
the waiting clients make room, for another
rising bunch of lifetime disposals. It is
the next round in the sing-song by treble touches,
a high start not detained by the option
of a dream to pass right on through
the spirit proof coming off the top. What
don't you want, is there no true end
to grief at joy, casting away deterrent hope
in a spate of root filling? The upside of the song
from the valley below excites lock-tremors
as the crest gets the voice right by proxy,
non-stick like a teflon throat. To press on
without fear of explanation, refusing the jab:
Ah Curly do your day is done, The course
of woe is quickly run. Low without loss
your shining heart Has nothing but the better
part. The star of swords is put upon
his neck. He falls to the ground. Why not?
It is a root and branch arrangement, giving
the keys openly to a provident reversal,
to net uptake. To these Whom we resist.
To blot out a shabby record by a daze
intrinsic in transit: *See what is won,*
We have cut him down, Like the evening sun
His only crown. Don't you think that's enough
to peel a larynx at a flotation, they say,
by the stub of a tuning fork delivery. The issue
hits all-time peaks in no time at all,
buy on the rumour, sell on the fact. Only
a part gives access to the rest, you get
in at the floor too: *And his dance is gone.*

TIM TROMPETER

TOM RAWORTH

I remember the Tower because my reading there was the first public reading I gave. It must have been some time in 1966 because my first book was not yet out. Stuart Montgomery drove me up, and I remember the car careering across a field by the motorway as he tried to turn off too fast. I remember people on the floor, or on old armchairs; and smoking a joint with Tom sitting on the *Wall*.

TOM RAWORTH/two untitled poems

experience – the sudden rush
of concentrated delusiveness
a race between sounds
the luminous, priceless
fumblings of uninstructed people
dimly aware how surprisingly
stable is soon to be shaky
in cycles, like stars
waiting till dawn
universally tired
altered past recognition
of personal individuality
shutting only ugliness out
when that sudden light comes

sight indeed seemed
unbidden and uninvited
before frost came
backed by luxury
from her barely opened mouth
painfully by his shoulder
in the direction
of the vast waxed hardwood floor
they heard his rib
smite her optic nerve
to jelly
a sound almost eerie
as death
passing through lips and nostrils

CAROL RUMENS

I was very nervous the night I read at Morden Tower. It was my first reading since coming to the North East. When I saw the size of the queue up the Tower steps I nearly ran away. But of course it was fantastic to read to such a large, keen, committed audience. Poets learn to live with indifference and cynicism, and forget how lovely it is to be received with enthusiasm. When I read at Morden Tower I felt in a way that poetry had begun all over again for me.

CAROL RUMENS/Jarrow

Nothing is left to dig, little to make.
Night has engulfed both firelit hall and sparrow.
Wind and car-noise pour across the Slake.
Nothing is left to dig, little to make
A stream of rust where a great ship might grow.
And where a union-man was hung for show,
Nothing is left to dig, little to make.
Night has engulfed both firelit hall and sparrow.

JON SILKIN

I think that the circular space contributed to a sense of intimate relation with the audience – an almost physical connection which I, at least, liked a great deal. I hope the Tower will receive better funding that it has recently, which will enable it to promote a greater range and diversity of poets.

JON SILKIN/The Levels

Past Quaking Houses,
on the bull-neck of the north Pennines, that has no head,
in a flat torn sky,
wind circling among hills, like a miner
with a wide shallow bowl, panning –
above Alston, I went with my nets
to dismal grass-blobbed flats, reaching
into the Solway's firth, soft basement
to rubbed, soft water
not poisoned yet by fission, where the fish frisk
in a dismal sort of way. Their tails lash
the brunette forms of the sea.

My nets an impediment over shoulders, catching
at knees, or scraping the back of calf and thigh.
On a journey not so big as a rushlight,
the bog's rushes smeared with sheep's fat,
I went. The quaker graveyard still scythed
of nettle and its remedy, dock. At Silloth
I threw my nets into the sea,
their meshes chagrined with a dead
exposure to air, and no fish.
Nets that weighed on me, hiss in the floating sea.
For hours, against the sea's pull
tugging like any fish's mouth, green flimsy
triangles of salt wrinkling greek characters
on sifting illiterate sand.

At length six fish obliged, as if for pity
flickering over meshes they can't pass. I pulled
them out gasping against the heft
of frigid water, with biting mouths,
scraping the element they leave.
And their doleful eyes and breathless gills
tricked of their pasture hang in bodies
laid by on the denser lingual
of a mudded slab.

The silence thickens
and turns to water: lives that bite
the shining levels of mud,
the creamy monstrous air, teeth that gnash it,
are dying. Teeth and eyes hook
with a presentiment of my death.
I have taken your lives –
delicate adroit netsman.

IAIN CRICHTON SMITH

I found Morden Tower had a curious atmosphere which was, in some way difficult to define, suitable to poetry. It was in no way opulent but its very bareness challenged the imagination to come to terms with it, to 'fill' it. In this sense I preferred it to richer venues. It reflected, it seems to me, the 'poverty' of poetry itself in a material sense, and seemed to be a true correlative of it.

IAIN CRICHTON SMITH/On the Golan Heights

On the Golan Heights there are unexploded mines
and the small red flowers grow around them.
The electronic fence will betray the nose of a dog.

Something is waiting for us in history like an unexploded mine,
like the crux of a scholarly book.

Though we bend over it in our black caps
though we sweep the sky like radar
it is waiting for us,
this terrible destiny.

It is in the stones, and among the flowers,
it is in the clouds, in the grass,
it is like a safe waiting to be opened.

Our destiny is dreadful and inevitable.

Our fate dressed in black crossing the golden field
when the mine like a bouquet explodes.

MOIRA CONWAY

KEN SMITH

The Tower, probably with Bête Noire in Hull the best venue to be asked to read at, down Muggers' Lane and up the stone steps in the wall to the stone room. Always a good audience, invariably a good gig. Long may she reign.

KEN SMITH/Running on Empty

What's it like? they ask.
Lots of space debris I reply: this music
has been written by psychologists.
'My name is Vera Lute, from Truth or Consequences.'

Some wander all their days
and never find the river.
So many lives are wasted and no one knows why.
That sounds to me like a crime.

Tell the BBC in confidence,
tell the golfing correspondent from *Angling Times*:
there were days when my heart was sore
and it always seemed to be raining.

Now there's too much to be angry about,
and no one left to forgive.
I'm the atheist at the bishop's conference.
I'm the fly in the ointment on the wall.

On and on down the dirty decades.
Nothing as described in the brochure,
as promised on the party platform
and nothing but bullshit to listen to.

My country is falling off the back of a lorry
but I bear you no malice, Alice.
What I'm in is chagrin. It's late,
I'm out on the road, running on empty.

And I'm calling you in.
I'm calling you in.

MARTIN STANNARD

I t was 'Poetry Live' all round Britain, and it was like most of the poets in the country with wit enough to catch a train without help were heading every which way in search of ever more remote and unlikely venues. Someone was trying to convince someone else that poetry really was alive. On the Inter-City to Newcastle, Brian Patten and I met over an 'Ambit' and swopped books. I'd already been slightly fazed by the idea of reading at Morden Tower, to be honest. Now, I simply know that every town should have its own version of the Tower. The audience was small, but warm (figuratively speaking), informed, and (I think) enthusiastic.

MARTIN STANNARD/Commercial

Dreaming of being
invisible

is enough to
wake anyone up, but

tonight there were
no dreams,

just the owls
screeching and you

hogging the quilt
making me cold.

When I
get up in the night to
go to the toilet a number
of animals scrabble at
the back door;

someone
should make a film of
our lives, for a
couple of minutes
at least.

It would be
a good commercial

for something nobody in
their right mind needs.

ANNE STEVENSON

I first encountered Morden Tower early in 1977, I think. I remember the train trip from Oxford and the dingy, smoky grandeur of Newcastle Station. It was my first visit to the North East, and I was dazed by a city different in almost every respect from Oxford. I recall an Indian meal, a noisy pub (more smoke) and then the scary, black back lane, glistening with rain, through which I was guided like a prisoner to the Tower. The top room, which I still think of as round, was badly lit in those days (as these?), and I can't remember that it was heated at all. People sat in their coats and listened silently while I read under the single naked bulb. The Tower's cheerful shabbiness was and is conducive to an important kind of subversion in Mammon's England. Morden Tower represents for me the spirit of living poetry in the North East.

ANNE STEVENSON/The Morden Angel

A monologue of the plaster bust of an angel who presides over poetry readings in the Morden Tower, Newcastle.

My sideways smile
means I'm wearing
the joke of my being
like a punishment.

The child of baroque
imagination, I could have
risen. In cloudy
theatrical surroundings,
say, with a pipe
on a ceiling, or burdened
with a wreath of pineapples,
my squint might not
have disadvantaged me.

But here, where the spirit of
Art, one winter,
snagged the poor career
of my creator, I came
into my little kingdom
crooked. If it was a
muse he needed
why did my maker
make me dumb?

I am full to the lips
with iambic pentameters.
In couplets I might have
inspired him. (What has come
to my attention as 'verse'
in these late days
he wouldn't have believed).

Especially my wings
are worrying. Ought they
to wave like an angel's
or flutter like Cupid's?
They pin me to the wall
like a target.

It's from trying to
fly away from this wall
or back into the wall
that my temper suffers.

Here come those poets again,
their inelegant wails!
If only my wings would work.
If only my smile could talk.

MATTHEW SWEENEY

Most improbable of reading venues, a near ruin, or so it seemed on that first, led walk down the alley by the City Wall. There was no light. The steps to the Tower had no rail, and were frozen over. And the nearest loo was back down those steps, in the pub. A memorable reading!

MATTHEW SWEENEY/The Desert

He wanted rim-bel-terfass and nothing else.
He wanted a space-shot of the desert.
He wanted that Algerian woman he'd known
years before, who'd fed him couscous,
with rosewater made by her own mother.
He'd had a male friend who taught there,
on an oasis – he wanted him back there,
arriving, in the small hours, once a year
with dates, and goat-cheese, and the strong
red wines that held their own in France.
He wanted to be able to visit him –
take the train from Algiers, a rucksack
with bacon and whiskey on his back,
no advance warning, no Arabic, no French –
and send a series of postcards to himself
till, one by one, they all arrived back.

'rim-bel-terfass: a stew made of gazelle meat, with Saharan truffles'
Larousse Gastronomique

GAEL TURNBULL

The Morden Tower is a place where, sometimes against all odds, the magic happens and the word and spirit become one – without which the sound of poetry in our time would lack at least one particular and enduring resonance. A tower, yes, as refuge and vantage point. Long may it thrive.

GAEL TURNBULL/The Office Required of Them (1815)

Among those broken down by poverty
or brutalised by vice, the moral affections
become cold and dull, and thus
there are multitudes of wretches
who for bread or gin are ready
to sell their children into misery, which
on a first introduction to the mine
struggle and scream with terror
though there are to be found persons
brutal enough to force them into compliance
so that after a few trials they become tame
and spiritless and yield themselves up
without noise or resistance
to any kind of slavery that it pleases
their masters to impose, with few
more than eight years old and many
considerably less, in strength
barely sufficient to perform the office
required of them which is to open the door
as the horses pass through and who
at this duty are compelled to linger
in solitude and darkness, so that
in wintertime they never see daylight
except on a Sunday for it has been discovered
that they can serve for thirteen hours a day
without perishing, condemned to this
with as little consideration
as is felt for the hinges and pulleys
of the doors at which they attend
where, when I first saw one open,
did not perceive by what means
until, looking behind, I beheld
a miserable little creature standing there
without light, silent and motionless,
resembling in the abjectness of its condition,
some reptile peculiar to the place.

ANNE WALDMAN

ANNE WALDMAN/I Quit

I quit the night you left, quit getting lost outside
I quit the machine for its discipline knowing more than I do
I quit Ati class for 2 hours my mind going to visualisation of lip to cunt
       to heart to bone
In a ribbon of mantra, I quit praying
I quit the music that blasted the ear
I quit a place of terror and it quit me
I joined to the hearth, the stones kept silent
I quit lying about time
I quit sleep when it obscured your intent
You intended to go out later, I quit thinking about it
I quit the calibrated afternoon
The moment the sun broke through clouds I quit
Then a storm came, get inside
I walked inside I quit worrying
I quit the last program of the a.m.
I quit the final Auvergne song
I quit driving all over town after midnight
I quit but the 'ahrbel gorung' kept wooing me
I quit the long embrace
I quit strategizing & left off all their names
The list is all right quit adding to it
I quit the time she kept waiting for
I quit her making an offer to speech & cream
I quit the Progressive magazine
I quit plastic for 3 days
I died in my denial of water because sustenance is a kind of feat
I quit seeing the point
I quit wearing the fertility charm it dragged my neck down but I never
       gave up on Africa
I kept dreaming you like spice
I quit you'd better be prepared to take over
Will I love you?
Quit your projection
I quit under pressure, under glass
I folded before the money ran out

I quit I told you I'd better have a back-up
Be my friend I won't quit yet
I quit it's difficult to describe
A rough outline is to be read syllable by syllable
I quit dialing you were never there
I quit staring out the window
Moon, clouds, I quit the fantasy
Stars, they look calm
I quit the careful approach I was impulsive then
I quit giving my palm to your ambition
I quit my own restoration
I quit, was this viewed as defeat?
And when you were there, static was intolerable
I stood on a 40 foot high scaffold peeling paint into my face
Then I quit working for experts
I quit I'm not complaining it was time for a change
Take one step back
Were you informed?
I use words for my own loss
I use words as my table, as a kind of shrine
I sweep over the care of the words
They take care of themselves
I sweep them under my demand
I command that they not quit the scenario
The sentence quits the page as it ends
I quit as a phantom of exteriority
A double negative remains evanescent
Don't linger with my thought to quit
I tell you it happened once
It happens again
And the speed of the transition, could it quit?
Would myself-as-object quit?
I quit the *sine qua non* of that experience
Could I keep harping on my conclusions?
Is the language ripe enough?
Is all the data in?

I quit the fragility of the 'real'
Writing without end, I quit trying to stop
Conceit gets the best of the one-who-quits
I quit an outward appearance
No outward appearance without light
Well I quit the light then
How could that be, I couldn't quit gleaming
I couldn't quit radiating
I kept hidden
I quit being a stoic
I quit nostalgia for your past
Insatiable compassion, how to quit
I quit stalling
I quit representing my total existence
I quit speculating about the event
It would happen, I would be there, I can't quit
I quit defining the problem
Linguists were going around in circles
Is speech a human phenomenon?
I quit for no good reason
The speech was boring in the sense of redundant
I quit to leave everything as it is
I quit by blending in my durations with the other durations
I could never stop

MIKE WILKIN

D own a narrow alley ideal for muggings and
mayhem, slipping on cobbles strewn with boozy
vomit and the shrivelled balloons of lust, one strode in
eager anticipation. And, onwards past the reek and bab-
ble of Chinese kitchens we Childe Rolands to the dark
tower came! When we got there (to the Morden Tower
that is) frequently it was only the scaldic heat of fiery
bards that kept us warm, there being a temperamental
heating system usually powerless to combat the medieval
chill. Nevertheless, poetry was our grail, and the Morden
Tower uniquely offered over twenty-five years a heady
brew. All praise to Connie and Tom Pickard and to the
others who have kept the Morden Tower alive and thriving.

MIKE WILKIN/*Tynescape*

Dislodging a massive stink
Of grease and metals,
A sweaty cacophony
Of dungarees and blunt caps
In a black torrent
Floods the canteen hill.

Through a lounging hour
The still cranes shoulder
Strident choirs of gulls,
Patient for spilt bait.

Noon light daubs gantries;
Scarves of river oils
Shiver against rusty hulls.
Ghosting blindly to the sea
Bloated shoals of blobs
Embrace beneath rotting piers.
Rousing the slumbering yard
Sad sirens abruptly weep.

HUGO WILLIAMS

My first reading at the Tower, under Tom Pickard, was one of the few occasions on which I have been freezing, exhausted, excited, drunk, stoned, happy, afraid and ill all at the same time, which is probably just the chronic state of being younger than one is now, because the last time I was there, with Brendan Cleary, I was only drunk, stoned, happy, excited and cold, so there does seem to be some sort of progression.

HUGO WILLIAMS/*Autobiography*

They had a knobble knees competition long ago.
I thoroughly enjoyed myself.
I didn't really.
I hated coming home and finding the words
'bandaged' and 'bloody' lying there.
I ran upstairs to fetch a mop
and my body fell back on the bed.

Descending against my will,
I blocked my own path. I obscured the view.
Books balanced on my head. I seemed to be astride
a hobby-horse of reference works,
Proverbs and Maxims of All Ages
flickering its pages in my face
to simulate the passage of time.

I shuffled down the passage with a tray
and hit my head on something hard.
I came to a standstill in the hall
and all my possessions
went hurtling past me down the waste shoot.
I stood out of sight behind a curtain
crying and laughing to myself
as a dust cart crept along the street.

JONATHAN WILLIAMS

I t was a pleasure for uncivilised Americans (who didn't know chaps from blokes) to read in the Morden Tower to ears as keen as those provided by Basil Bunting, Sid Chaplin, Gordon Brown, Tom Pickard, Malcolm Rutherford, Peter Stattersfield, and the others. It was a place for chamber music under siege, a place in which you could avoid academic pomposities and the poetry societies' demand for Real Poetry. After four decades, I have no interest in reading aloud to any group in Britain that exists outside my parlour or my garden. Epicurus, Priapus, and Orpheus counsel: stay home! Which will be patent nonsense to those new unabashed boys and girls Mr Bunting always hoped for.

JONATHAN WILLIAMS/Three Dales Limericks

There was an old raven of Tarset
where n'ornithologists still cannot class it.
He stole like a lord
and he used such a word
that a dowager kicked him up t'arse sett.

There was an old boy of Bellingham
who sat in t'pub and said 'Ba goom,
you bugger, you bloke, you bugger,
you bugger, you bloke, you bugger...'
and nowt word else till Kingdom come.

There was an old knitter of Dent
whose sock was so long that it went
quite funny in the middle
and often filled with piddle
and was of no use for the rent.

CONTRIBUTORS

FLEUR ADCOCK was born in New Zealand and emigrated here in 1963. From 1979 to 1981 she lived in Newcastle upon Tyne where she was Northern Arts Literary Fellow. Her 'Selected Poems' (OUP) includes work from six previous books, and her most recent collection is 'The Incident Book' (OUP, 1986).

GILLIAN ALLNUTT was born in London in 1949. She has published 'Spitting the Pips Out' (Sheba, 1981) and 'Beginning the Avocado' (Virago, 1987), and co-edited 'The New British Poetry' (Paladin, 1988). Formerly Poetry Editor of City Limits magazine, she is a part-time teacher by trade.

PETER ARMSTRONG was born in 1957 at Blaydon on Tyne. He studied Philosophy and English at Sunderland, and began writing in the late seventies. His poems were included in the Bloodaxe anthology 'Ten North-East Poets' (1980) and his first solo collection, 'Risings', was published by Enitharmon in 1989. Married with two children, he now works as a psychiatric nurse.

PETER BENNET organised the Morden Tower programmes from 1984 to 1986. His publications include 'Sky-riding' (Peterloo), 'A Clee Sequence' (Lincs and Humberside Arts), and 'The Border Hunt' (Jackson's Arm). He has been a prizewinner in the National Poetry Competition and the Arvon/ Sotheby's International Poetry Competition, and won the Basil Bunting Award in 1987.

MICHAEL BLACKBURN was born in 1954 in County Durham, read English at Leeds University and now lives in Lincoln. His work has appeared in numerous magazines. He is the founder-editor of Jackson's Arm Press and 'Sunk Island Review'. Four collections of his poetry have been published, including 'Why Should Anyone Be Here And Singing?' and 'The Lean Man Shaving'.

PETE BROWN was a professional poet from 1960 to 1967, making a living from readings, and as a song-writer he was responsible for many Cream hits. He was a singer himself from 1968, leading the bands Battered Ornaments, Piblokto etc. He left the music business for a while to concentrate on screenwriting. He is now back in music, producing records and songwriting.

BASIL BUNTING was born in Newcastle upon Tyne in 1900 and educated at a Quaker public school and LSE. He was imprisoned as a conscientious objector during the First World War. In the twenties he assisted Ford Madox Ford on the 'Transatlantic Review' and his poems were included in Ezra Pound's 'Active Anthology' (1933). He lived abroad for many years – in Italy, and during the Second World War in Persia, where he was Vice-Consul at Isfahan. From the fifties onwards he worked as a sub-editor on the Newcastle 'Evening Chronicle'. Towards the end of his life he was Northern Arts Literary Fellow at the Universities of Newcastle and Durham, and also held posts at universities in the United States. His 'Collected Poems' appeared firstly from Fulcrum Press in 1968, and then in 1978 from OUP. Basil Bunting died in 1985.

RICHARD CADDEL was born in Bedford in 1949, and came to the North East as a music student in 1968. He is currently European Documentation Centre Librarian at Durham University Library. His published work includes 'Sweet Cicely' (2nd ed. Galloping Dog Press, 1988), 'Against Numerology' (North & South, 1988), and 'Uncertain Time' (Galloping Dog Press, 1990).

MATTHEW CALEY's first two collections 'Hicks' (Echo Room Press) and '13' (Jackson's Arm) both appeared in 1986. He has given many readings and a selection of his poems was broadcast on Radio 4 in 1988. He has published four more collections, the most recent being 'Channelhopper' (Echo Room Press).

GEORGE CHARLTON was born in Gateshead in 1950, and now lives in Newcastle, where he teaches in further education. In 1984 he was joint winner of the first Newcastle 'Evening Chronicle' poetry competition. A pamphlet, 'The Lost Boys', was published by the Echo Room Press in 1986, and his first book of poems, 'Nightshift Workers', was published by Bloodaxe in 1989.

BRENDAN CLEARY was born in 1958 in Co. Antrim, Ireland. He has published many booklets and his first full-length collection, 'White Bread and ITV', is due early in 1990 from Wide Skirt Press. He is the editor of 'The Echo Room' magazine, a part-time lecturer and performance poet. He organised Morden Tower readings for three-and-a-half years, until the end of 1989.

BOB COBBING is a concrete, visual and sound poet, with over a hundred publications and some thirty records and tapes. He has participated in all the international Sound Poetry Festivals, and has worked with improvising musicians such as Paul Burwell (abAna) and Hugh Metcalfe (BirdYak). He is a publisher of experimental poetry under the Writers' Forum imprint.

TONY CURTIS was born in Carmarthen in 1946. He teaches Creative Writing at the Polytechnic of Wales. His 'Selected Poems' appeared in 1986 and his latest collection is 'The Last Candles' (Seren Books, 1989). He has written on Abse and Heaney and 'How to Study Modern Poetry' (Macmillan) appears in 1990.

IVOR CUTLER was born in Glasgow. For many years he earned his living in education, among other things teaching music, African drumming, movement, drama and poetry to 7-11 year-olds. He has published four children's books including 'Meal One' (Heinemann). His poetry collections include 'Many Flies Have Feathers' (Trigram), 'Private Habits' (Arc), and 'A Nice Wee Present from Scotland' (Arc).

CAROL ANN DUFFY's most recent collections are 'Standing Female Nude' (Anvil Press, 1985) and 'Selling Manhattan' (Anvil Press, 1987) which received the Somerset Maugham Award. A new collection is due from Anvil in the spring of 1990.

HELEN DUNMORE was born in 1952 in Beverley, Yorkshire. After graduating from York University in 1973, she worked in Finland for two years, and now lives in Bristol. She has published three books of poems with Bloodaxe: 'The Apple Fall' (1983), 'The Sea Skater' (1986), and 'The Raw Garden' (1988), a Poetry Book Society Choice.

PAUL DURCAN was born in Dublin in 1944, of Co. Mayo parents. He studied at University College, Cork, and in 1974 won the Patrick Kavanagh Award. His most recent books are 'Going Home to Russia' (Blackstaff Press, Belfast, 1987), and 'Jesus and Angela' (Blackstaff, 1988).

ALISTAIR ELLIOT was born in Liverpool in 1932 and has been living in Newcastle since 1967. His first book, 'Contentions', was published by Ceolfrith Press, Sunderland, in 1977 and his collected poems ('My Country') was published recently by Carcanet.

ROY FISHER was born in 1930 in Birmingham. His 'Poems 1955-1987' and 'A Furnace' are published by OUP.

ALLEN GINSBERG was born in Newark, New Jersey, in 1926. A close friend of William Burroughs, Neal Cassady and Jack Kerouac, he was associated with the Beat movement and the San Francisco Renaissance in the fifties. His first volume of poetry, 'Howl and Other Poems', appeared in 1956 and he has published prolifically ever since. His 'Collected Poems' came out in paperback in 1989.

LEE HARWOOD was born in 1939 and grew up in Chertsey, Surrey. He has published fifteen books of poetry and several volumes of translation. His most recent collection is 'Crossing the Frozen River: Selected Poems' (Paladin, 1988).

GEOFF HATTERSLEY was born in 1956 in Wombwell, South Yorkshire. He now lives with his wife in Huddersfield, where he edits 'The Wide Skirt' magazine and press and runs writers' workshops for Kirklees Metropolitan Council. His publications include 'Shadows on the Beach' (Red Sharks Press, 1987) and 'Port of Entry' (Littlewood Press, 1989).

SEAMUS HEANEY is the author of several books of poetry, most recently 'The Haw Lantern' (Faber, 1987). In 1988 he published a book of critical prose, 'The Government of the Tongue' (Faber), and at present is preparing a sequence of poems provisionally entitled 'Squarings'.

LIBBY HOUSTON was born in North London, grew up in the West Country, and read English at Oxford. Her books include 'At the Mercy' (1981) and, most recently, 'Necessity' (Slow Dancer, 1988). Since 1973 she has been regularly commissioned to write poems for children for BBC Schools, and a collection of these, 'All Change', is due from OUP during 1990.

TONY JACKSON writes: "'Painted Walls' is the first piece of public poetry I have written in years, and therefore the first I've allowed to be published in a long while. I actually dreamt it only a few days before being asked for something for this anthology. True. At the moment I'm working on an 'Investigation' called 'Dead Fishes', my first long piece since 'Hot Novels'. As ever I am always looking for an agent, publisher or both."

RICHARD KELL spent his early childhood in India and was educated in Belfast and Dublin. In 1983 he retired from his job as a senior lecturer in English Literature at Newcastle Polytechnic to spend more time on writing. He has published several collections, most recently 'In Praise of Warmth' (Dedalus Press, Dublin, 1987).

AUGUST KLEINZAHLER was born in New Jersey in 1949. His poetry has appeared in 'The New Yorker', 'Ploughshares' and many other magazines. His first book was 'Storm Over Hackensack' (Moyer Bell, NY, 1985) and his second, 'On Johnny's Time', was published in this country by Pig Press, Durham in 1988. August Kleinzahler lives in San Francisco.

TOM LEONARD was born in Glasgow in 1944. His collection 'Intimate Voices: Writing 1965-83' was joint winner of the Saltire Society Book of the Year Award in 1984, a few weeks before Scottish Central Regional Council banned it from their school libraries. Further publications have been 'Situations Theoretical and Contemporary' (Galloping Dog Press) and 'Satires and Profanities' (Scottish TUC).

LIZ LOCHHEAD's books of poems are 'Memo for Spring', 'Islands' and 'The Grimm Sisters', all of which are included in 'Dreaming Frankenstein and Collected Poems'. She has been a frequent writer of and contributor to theatrical revues, and has published a collection of song lyrics, monologues and raps, 'True Confessions'. She lives in Glasgow.

NORMAN MacCAIG was born in Edinburgh and read Classics at Edinburgh University. He taught in a number of schools in that city, and finished up as Reader in Poetry at Stirling University. He has published sixteen books of poems of which the latest two are 'Voice-over' and 'Collected Poems'.

HUGH MacDIARMID was the pseudonym of Christopher Murray Grieve, who was born in 1892 in Langholm, Dumfriesshire. He planned to become a teacher but abandoned this for journalism which gave him scope for the expression of his left-wing politics. During the First World War he served in the RAMC, after which he worked as a journalist in Scotland and England. After a breakdown in health he retreated to a croft on Whalsay, in the Shetlands, where he lived in poverty. He worked as an engineer on the Clyde during the Second World War, afterwards settling at Biggar, Lanarkshire with his second wife. He lived there until his death in 1978. The two-volume 'Complete Poems of Hugh MacDiarmid' is published by Martin Brian & O'Keeffe and Penguin.

IAN McMILLAN was born in 1956 and has been a freelance writer since 1981. He has published many collections including 'Selected Poems' (Carcanet, 1987), 'Unselected Poems' (Wide Skirt Press, 1988) and 'More Poems Please Waiter and Quickly!' (Sow's Ear Press, 1988). He has performed all over the country, both solo and with Circus of Poets.

BARRY MacSWEENEY was born in Newcastle upon Tyne in 1948. Since leaving school at sixteen he has worked as an investigative journalist and news editor on various newspapers and is currently deputy editor on the Shields Gazette. He lives in Newcastle. Widely published both here and abroad, his books include 'Fool's Gold', 'Odes' and 'Ranter'.

WILLIAM MARTIN was born in Silksworth, County Durham, in 1925, and left school at fourteen. He served in the RAF, 1943-46, ending up in India, and then worked in the Health Service for thirty years, as an Audiology Technician. His collections are 'Easthope' (Ceolfrith), 'Tidings of Our Bainsea' (Wearmouth Festival), 'Crackenrigg' (Taxus) and 'Hinny Beata' (Taxus).

ADRIAN MITCHELL was born in London in 1932. The poems he performs are mostly in 'For Beauty Douglas', 'On the Beach at Cambridge', 'Love Songs of World War Three' and 'Nothingmas Day' (Allison & Busby). He has also written four novels, many original plays with songs for both children and adults, and has translated/adapted classic foreign plays.

GERALDINE MONK was born in Blackburn in 1952 and is now based in Sheffield. Her publications include 'Tiger Lilies' (Rivelin Press, 1982), 'Sky Scrapers' (Galloping Dog, 1986) and 'Herein Lie Tales of Two Inner Cities' (Writers' Forum, 1986).

VINCE MORRISON was born in Sunderland in 1952. His poems have appeared in many magazines and anthologies. He was one of the contributors to '2 Poets and an Illustrator' (Wearmouth 1300 Festival, 1974) and 'Ten North-East Poets' (Bloodaxe, 1980). His pamphlet 'The Season of Comfort' was published by Bloodaxe in 1979.

ERIC MOTTRAM's 'Selected Poems' (North & South, 1989) contains work from sixteen books published 1971-1989, and his most recent collection is 'Peace Projects and Brief Novels' (Talus, 1989). His prose books include 'The Wild Good and the Hard Ultimately' on Allen Ginsberg. He is Professor of English and American Literature at King's College, University of London.

HENRY NORMAL was born in Nottingham in 1956, and is still recoiling from the anticlimax.

JEFF NUTTALL was born in Lancashire in 1933. He made his living as an art teacher until 1984 when he retired from his position as Head of Fine Art at Liverpool Polytechnic. He has published over thirty books of fiction, verse, social observation and graphics, most recently 'The Pleasures of Necessity' (Arrowspire) and 'Mad With Music' (Writers' Forum).

SEAN O'BRIEN was born in 1952 and grew up in Hull. He is currently Fellow in Creative Writing at the University of Dundee. His collections of poems are 'The Indoor Park' (Bloodaxe, 1983) and 'The Frighteners' (Bloodaxe, 1987). A selection of recent poems is contained in the pamphlet 'Boundary Beach' (The Honest Ulsterman, 1989).

CONNIE PICKARD was born on Tyneside and spent her childhood in a Durham mining village. She was educated at King's College, Dunelm, in the 1950s. In 1964 she co-founded Morden Tower poetry-reading centre and co-organised readings there until 1976. She published, with Tom Pickard and Richard Hamilton, the magazine 'King Ida's Watch Chain' which was dedicated to Basil Bunting, and in the same year, 1965, his long poem 'The Spoils'. She now lives and writes in Gateshead.

TOM PICKARD, born in 1946, works as a writer and film maker. His most recent book is 'We Make Ships' (Secker & Warburg, 1989) and his most recent film 'Tell Them in Gdansk' (Channel 4, 1989). His latest collection of poems is 'Custom and Exile' (Allison & Busby, 1986).

J.H. PRYNNE's most substantial collection is 'Poems' (Agneau 2, 1982) and his most recent is 'Word Order' (Prest Roots Press, 1989).

TOM RAWORTH's first collection of poems was 'The Relation Ship' (Goliard, 1966). He has since then published more than twenty books including 'A Serial Biography' (Fulcrum, 1969/Turtle Island, 1977), and 'Tottering State: New and Selected Poems' (Paladin, 1988).

CAROL RUMENS was born in London and writes poetry, fiction and drama. Her 'Selected Poems' and her first novel, 'Plato Park', appeared from Chatto in 1987. In 1988 Bloodaxe Books published 'The Greening of the Snow Beach', the outcome of a visit to Russia in 1987. Her most recent book is 'From Berlin to Heaven' (Chatto, 1989).

JON SILKIN was born in London in 1930. He co-edits the literary quarterly 'Stand Magazine' which he founded in 1952. He has published nine collections of poetry, the two most recent being 'The Ship's Pasture' (1986) and 'Selected Poems' (1988). He edited 'The Penguin Book of First World War Poetry' and co-edited 'The Penguin Book of First World War Prose' (1989).

IAIN CRICHTON SMITH was born in 1928 on the Isle of Lewis. He is bilingual in English and Gaelic and has written novels, poems, short stories and plays in both languages. His latest collection of poems, 'The Village and Other Poems' is due from Carcanet, and his latest novel, 'The Dream', from Macmillan.

KEN SMITH was born in East Yorkshire in 1938, and lives in London. He has published several books including 'Fox Running', 'The Poet Reclining', 'Burned Books', 'Terra', 'A Book of Chinese Whispers' and 'Wormwood', all from Bloodaxe, and 'Inside Time' from Harrap.

MARTIN STANNARD was born in 1952 and lives in Suffolk with his wife and two sons. He currently works at Ipswich Museum as Community Arts Worker. His collections include 'The Flat of the Land' (Wide Skirt Press, 1987) and 'The Gracing of Days: New and Selected Poems' (Slow Dancer, 1989). 'Denying England' is due from Wide Skirt early in 1990.

ANNE STEVENSON is an American poet who has lived most of her adult life in Britain. She was Northern Arts Literary Fellow 1981-82 and again 1985-86. Her 'Selected Poems' was published by OUP in 1987, and in paperback in 1989. 'Bitter Fame', her biography of Sylvia Plath, appeared recently.

MATTHEW SWEENEY was born in Donegal in 1952 and has lived in London for some years. He has held various writing fellowships and won the Prudence Farmer Prize in 1984 and a Cholmondeley Award in 1987. His collection 'Blue Shoes' was published by Secker & Warburg in 1989.

GAEL TURNBULL was born in Edinburgh in 1928, and now lives there again after spending most of his life in England, Canada and the US. His most recent publications include 'A Gathering of Poems 1950-1980' (Anvil Press Poetry), 'Spaces' (Satis) and 'A Winter Journey' (Pig Press).

ANNE WALDMAN has an international reputation as a reader-performer. Featuring her own work, she performs coast-to-coast in the US as well as throughout Europe. Formerly director of the Poetry Project at St Mark's Church-in-the-Bowery in New York, she has published ten books of poetry, the latest being 'Blue Mosque' (United Artists, 1987).

MIKE WILKIN was born in Stanley, a small pit town ten miles from Newcastle, and currently lives at Cullercoats near the mouth of the Tyne. He has been published in various little magazines and was one of the 'Ten North-East Poets', an anthology published by Bloodaxe Books in 1980.

HUGO WILLIAMS was born in 1942, and is married with one daughter. He has published two travel books, one of which was 'No Particular Place to Go' about his adventures in the US. Also several books of poetry including 'Writing Home', a selected poems, and 'Self-Portrait With a Slide', due out in June 1990. He is poetry editor of the New Statesman.

JONATHAN WILLIAMS has been occupied publishing the 105 books of The Jargon Society and dozens of his own volumes since he began at Black Mountain College in 1951. Some recent titles are 'Blackbird Dust' (essays); 'Metafours for Mysophobes' (poems); and 'Quantulumcumque: The Least That Can Be Said' (poems). He spends half of the year in a cottage in Dentdale, Cumbria.